## *What others are saying . . .*

Kristin weaves threads of hope and humor throughout an authentic representation of the challenges endured on her adoption journey. Kristin's writing is a perfect blend of authenticity and hope wrapped refreshingly in humor.

> — Michele Schneidler, Pastor of Orphan Care,
> Overlake Christian Church

*Born Broken* is an invaluable resource for anyone who is caring for a child who comes from a traumatic background. Kristin's real-life examples, heart-felt stories, and practical advice are the perfect recipe for hope on this journey.

> — Ira J. Chasnoff, MD, President, NTI Upstream

Once I started reading *Born Broken*, I couldn't put it down. I felt I was walking through Kristin's story, and in some small way, she was walking through mine. Kristin would understand my family like very few people can. Kristin weaves a beautiful tapestry of honesty, raw emotion, and hope into a single book. I highly recommend *Born Broken* to everyone parenting a child with a history of trauma and to anyone walking alongside them.

> — Lisa Qualls, Mom by birth, adoption, and foster care
> Writer/Speaker/Encourager at onethankfulmom.com

Riveting and heartfelt, Kristin Berry's *Born Broken* is a must-read for adoptive and foster families and the people who support them. With a spirit of vulnerability and well-written prose, Kristin boldly shares the ups and downs of the Berry's journey to becoming the family God had always planned. Don't miss the beautiful honesty and encouragement of this book!

> — Cherie Lowe, author of *Slaying the Debt Dragon:*
> *How One Family Conquered Their Money Monster*
> *and Found an Inspired Happily Ever After*

I couldn't put this book down. I felt her pain, crying when she talked about lying in bed with her son before they had to take him to residential. I thought about my children as babies and what it would be like to make that kind of decision. So much pain and loneliness. She helps you see the love she has for her son, and it broke my heart when he began to hurt her. I never once felt anger toward her son. My heart hurt for him too because I could understand that this was not her son, but his disability. I knew this story and lived through it all as her best friend, never truly understanding or feeling her pain like I did when I read this book. The love and hope she has for Alex is what every mother feels.

— Nicole Goerges, wife and mother of five

As an adult adoptee, and a person with a vested interest in adoption and foster care, I can say that Kristin's words on the subject of trauma are powerful, true, and healing. This is a must-read if you're on the adoption journey, or simply a parent who is raising a child from a traumatic past.

— Tony Wolf, author, speaker, and comedian

# Born Broken

## AN ADOPTIVE JOURNEY

Kristin Berry

First printing: April 2017

New Leaf Press is a division of the New Leaf Publishing Group, Inc.

ISBN: 978-0-89221-754-0
ISBN: 978-1-61458-589-3 (digital)
Library of Congress Number: 2017902087

Cover by Diana Bogardus

Please consider requesting that a copy of this volume be purchased by your local library system.

**Printed in the United States of America**

Please visit our website for other great titles:
www.newleafpress.com

For information regarding author interviews,
please contact the publicity department at (870) 438-5288.

**New Leaf Press**
A Division of New Leaf Publishing Group
www.newleafpress.com

# Contents

# Preface

This book was written with permission from my son. I wrote this book hesitantly, afraid that I would hurt my son with my words, always afraid that I would not protect my son's dignity. Each word was written with his blessing. When the story was too hard to write he urged me to keep writing, and his wish is this:

> Mom, you need to write the truth. It is hard to live with FASD. I hate that I have hurt people. I hate that school is hard. I hate that I always make the wrong choice. I hate living like this. People need to know what this is like. People need to know that drinking while they are pregnant is never okay. People need to know.

This book is dedicated to my son. He is the strongest person I know.

CHAPTER 1

# Heartbeat

*His heart is beating — just a flutter really. Undetectable, unseen, growing each day. She doesn't know he's there yet. She suspects though. Each time she comes down from her euphoric high, the reality lingers at the fringe of her consciousness. She pops the tab on one more can of beer and dulls the reality. She's going to be a mother.*

## An Ill-Prepared Life

The first time I knew of him, it was Christmastime. He was just barely realized, not yet born, with a fate that lay undecided. His mom knew he was coming and raced against the clock to find enough money for an abortion. She hesitated though each time she spoke of the possibility. Haltingly, she weighed the choice that lay before her. I too laid awake at night thinking about her choice. Something about this unborn child filled my heart with the deepest love and longing. I prayed each day for his safe arrival. In the end, she chose life but not sobriety. The following spring, she gave birth to a 4 lb. 2 oz. baby boy. Relief washed over me when I learned of his birth. He had an uphill battle but he was already a fighter. He clawed his way out of the NICU and into the arms of a mother who wasn't quite ready.

*They left the hospital and returned to the women's shelter.*
*She had the gifts of strangers to rely on to care for her child.*
*The other women patted his head and took turns holding*
*him. She was appreciative of their attention, but as she*
*returned to the room she shared with three other women,*
*she knew she was ultimately alone. With a premature son*
*and a preschool daughter at her side, she knew she had to*
*start thinking of the future. She laid the child to sleep in his*
*borrowed crib and wandered about what the future held.*
*She was nearing her 30-day limit at the shelter. Her time*
*there had been extended, but soon she would have to find a*
*place for them to stay. She knew the father of her children*
*was not the best choice for any of them. He was a kind*
*person at heart who was caught in the same cycle of sobriety*
*and relapse as she. It was dangerous to go back. She knew*
*this, even as she lay down beside her little ones. Placing a*
*pillow over her ears to drown out the constant murmur*
*of the crowded building, she fell asleep with her new plan*
*confirmed. In the morning she would return to him.*

I knew of his story through a mutual friend, and I thought of him often that first year of his life. The first time I saw him he was six months old, just a tiny little ball of energy. His mom and I talked about the weather and our two daughters. We compared their spunky laughs and the colors of their hair. My daughter's deep black against her daughter's honey-colored highlights. She told me she once lived in a little Ohio town. I shared that it was just a few miles from where I had grown up. We each smiled with the joy of someone finding a connection. Sometimes it's the most trivial things that bind us to others. In one such meeting, we shared the usual small exchanges. Without cause and without much thought she blurted out a secret. "I think it's nice that your daughter is adopted. I grew up in 13 foster homes, but my mom would never let me go. I always wished I had a family." I could think of nothing more profound, so uttered a soft, "Oh." We changed topics and eventually waved goodbye as acquaintances often do. She had no reason to think often of me, but I thought of her story and her son each day.

Our paths didn't cross again for the rest of the year. A mutual friend and I would meet each Sunday for a time of prayer. It was during that time that I learned that the baby who had grabbed my heart was once again facing uncertainty. His mom had found herself in trouble again and was at risk of losing both of her children.

*The week she took the pregnancy test, she also failed a random drug screen. She and her baby's father would lose their transitional housing within the week. She would once again wait to be admitted to the shelter. They would require sobriety too, and the fear of a day without using gripped her heart. Pressing on her shoulders was also the thought of sleeping outside in the winter with two small children. She tried to stay clean through the rest of the week and so did the father. They were agitated and restless. One night as she fixed a tuna sandwich for her little girl and a bottle for her son, the tension snapped. The baby was on a blanket on the floor screaming wildly, the preschool daughter was pacing in the kitchen waiting on her meal. The father cupped his hands over his ears and yelled at the mother. She dropped the sandwich and pushed him yelling at him to get out. He reached over and grabbed the baby from his blanket as the pitch of his yelps reached painful heights. Realizing the danger, she tried to lower her own voice and reach the baby. It was too late. Her son was tossed against the nearest wall with a sickening thud. The little girl stood in the kitchen wide-eyed with hands over her ears. The next hour was a flurry of police, paramedics, and caseworkers. The little boy sustained nothing but a bruise; the little girl lost her will to talk. The father spent the night in jail, the mother was once again on the radar of child protective services, and none of them ever stepped foot in that home again.*

## Two Stories Become One

That same January, I was sitting at my kitchen table, watching the snow pile into thick mounds along the gravel driveway. I pondered the difficulty of getting my car out of the driveway for a quick trip to the grocery store. A cardinal, perched on the stark, leafless tree caught my attention. I clasped the hand of my tiny daughter, Joelle, and pointed her finger toward it. "Oh," she exclaimed, "pretty."

Just then, the phone rang, breaking that morning's silence. I picked up on the third ring, perplexed at the number I saw on the ID. It was the little boy's mother. Why was she calling me? We really weren't that close. "Hello," I said, a little too loudly. Quietly, she mispronounced my name. I sensed her mustering up the courage to say something difficult. And then she did. "Um, I'm pregnant . . . again. . . and I know your daughter is adopted. I was just wondering, you know, um, would you consider adopting my baby?" I sucked in a quick breath. *Calm down,* I told myself, *I know you're eager but don't be too eager.* I longed for another baby; my heart was pounding so loudly I thought she must hear it over the phone. "Why don't you tell me what's going on," I said in my best calm-voice. She spent the next 30 minutes telling me about being homeless, her baby's father, and her struggle to provide for her other two children. "I just can't do it again," she sobbed.

"I understand," I whispered. I didn't really, but I could feel the hurt in her words. I looked at my toddler and thought about toting her into a homeless shelter. I imagined us begging for food or a warm place to sleep. "I will do what I can to help," I promised as I hung up the phone.

I spent the next few minutes mesmerized by the falling snow. Feelings so raw, they were too difficult to feel. I gave into numbness. My daughter seemed to sense this need for silence as she sat perched in her high chair, examining the bright red cardinal and his counterpart searching the lawn for the seed we had scattered.

A knock at the door, snapped me back into reality. I rose to answer it, remembering I had agreed to watch my neighbor's son.

She stood at the bottom of my porch steps next to her son's wheelchair. As I helped her carry him through the front door, I blurted out, "Someone just asked me to adopt a baby." Hands frozen from the cold, heart frozen from the reality, I couldn't get either to work as I fumbled with the tie to her son's knit hat.

"What?" she said. "Are you serious?" I could always count on this friend to bring a proper amount of emotion to the craziness of this life. She slipped off her son's coat, unbuckled him from the wheelchair, and sat down on my couch. I gathered my daughter from her high chair, and plopped her next to her little friend as I sat on the chair facing my friend. As a fellow adoptive mom, I knew I had a safe place to share, and I did. Abruptly, in the middle of our conversation, she stopped and prayed over this hurting mother. She prayed over me. And she prayed over the three children whose lives lay in the balance of this one important decision. Before she got up to go she fished the number of an adoption lawyer from the bottom of her large purse. I tucked it into my pocket as I waved goodbye.

For the rest of that chilly day, I watched two precious babies play together and imagined a tiny baby beside them. At naptime, I wandered through the house and envisioned a new little one. *Here is where I'll put the rocking chair. Here is where the crib will go.* My thoughts were of nothing else. I knew it was a long shot. Babies don't just fall in your lap. I couldn't help it though. My arms longed to hold this new baby. My heart still ached for the little boy and his sister in peril, wandering in the cold.

My husband, Mike, arrived home that night and scooped up his baby girl. Tossing her in the air, Joelle giggled and smiled. I couldn't quite find the words to describe what had happened that day. We continued our evening without so much as a word of that day's events. Sometimes I find that when I have the most to say, I simply can't say a thing. That night as I folded my jeans neatly on my dresser, the piece of paper slipped out. "You'll never guess who called today," I began. "Remember my friend? You know, the one with the little girl and the little boy. She is pregnant again and wants to talk to us about adopting the baby." I couldn't quite gauge his reaction at first. He had a lot of questions and listened carefully to the story. In the end he agreed that it would be a good idea to meet with her and with the lawyer to see if this was even a possibility for our family.

We spent the next few weeks updating our home study. We met with the lawyer and formulated a hypothetical plan. As things began to fall into place we became cautiously hopeful. When she called to tell us that the baby was a girl, we really began to believe that this might happen. We knew that this was such a tough decision and a sacrifice for our friend. We settled on the name Zoe. *Zoe* means *life*, and we referred to her as "Zoe" in our own conversations. We felt that despite her uncertain future, Zoe was a name that honored her life as well as her birth mother.

My dreams were filled with visions of the little boy and his big sister. My heart was brimming with the hope of another new life.

# CHAPTER 2

# Bad News

In early March, I was curled up on my favorite oversized chair. I wrapped the worn quilt tighter around my shoulders to brace against the late winter chill. The sound of rain tapped against the glass directly behind my head as the theme to the late night show played softly on the TV. My eyes were heavy with impending sleep. I vowed not to nod off on the couch, but with each passing moment the lull of the rain overtook my resolve. As my eyes began to submit, I was jolted awake by the shrill ring of the telephone. Noting the time, I answered with concern in my voice. The sound on the other end was a near hysterical wailing. "They took them! They took them!" I sat up straight, my blanket falling to the floor.

"Who? Who took them? What did they take?" I couldn't understand anything that was happening. I bolted to the caller ID. It was the little boy's mom. "Oh no! Okay, take a deep breath and tell me what's going on. Is it the kids? Are you okay? Is the baby okay?" I forced myself to take a deep breath as well and allowed her to share her story.

She and the children had returned to the shelter when they exhausted the kindness of family and friends. The shelter required random drug screens, and she had failed another one earlier that afternoon. The staff could no longer give extra chances and had to file a report. Child Services had been at the shelter that day. It was the final straw for them and the children had been deemed CHINS (child in need of services). A new case would be opened. All she knew was that the little girl had gone to emergency shelter care, and the little boy would spend the first part of this process in a foster home. "Please, will you please take them? I know it's a lot to ask, but I can't have them with strangers."

I took one more deep breath and responded with what I knew was right in my heart. "Yes, of course we will. Try to get some rest. We'll figure all of this out." I hung up the phone and tiptoed into my bedroom. I crawled silently between the sheets to find that my husband was wide awake.

"What was that all about?" he asked. He stayed awake to hear the whole story. As we fell asleep that night, we were in agreement. We needed to help.

The following morning, we set out to call the Department of Child Services. I had the name of the caseworker along with every hurried detail I had gathered from the night before. I was a woman on a mission. As it turned out, DCS didn't care about my mission. I couldn't even get past the front desk receptionist without security clearance on the level of the FBI. When I began crying about the children being separated and all alone, she hung up on me. I spent the rest of the day chasing my tail. I contacted the foster care licensing agency, left an email for the caseworker, called the little boy's mother, and finally called my own mother. I spilled my every frustration to her. She listened intently to the story and then said, "I've been praying the whole time you were talking. I don't know what you are supposed to do, but have you talked to your sister yet?" I practically smacked myself in the forehead. My sister was a caseworker for DCS in a county in northern Ohio. She wouldn't know the laws specific to my state, but she would have a better idea of how the system works. I couldn't believe I hadn't thought of that.

After a long conversation with my sister, and another page filled with directions, I felt armed to face the situation again. I made more headway the second time around. I learned how to get our license. I signed up for classes and even found a sympathetic license worker who fast-tracked our home study. I was on a roll again. Within the week we were well on our way to meeting the requirements to become a foster home. We were proud and surprised about our progress, but even as we moved forward, each new day began with the stark reminder that the little boy was in a foster home far away from his mom, dad, and big sister.

Four weeks later, we were in the thick of transforming our home. We had been a family of three for the past two years, and within weeks we hoped to become a family of six. We couldn't afford to wait. We moved bedrooms around, borrowed a crib and a toddler bed from a friend, and even updated the paint for the new baby's nursery. We spent every waking moment working on preparing for our new arrivals. I gave extra special care to the little boy's room. He had been growing in my heart since before he was born. I was thankful to be needed, but I couldn't have known how badly he would need me.

## More Bad News

Not only were we planning for the little boy and his big sister, we were preparing for an adoption as well. I cautiously set up the crib next to my side of the bed. I wanted to be the one to pat her sweet forehead if she fussed. I envisioned myself lifting her carefully from her bassinette and shuffling to the kitchen to warm a bottle. My arms longed to hold her. My fingers ached to run through her soft fine hair. We knew that so many things were uncertain, but still we hoped that we would soon be holding our new baby girl. Each day we navigated through the murky waters of foster parenting, we clung to the hope that we would be present at our newest daughter's birth. According to her mom and dad, we were to come straight to the hospital when she was born. They wanted us to hold her as soon as possible. We were so grateful to be included in the birth plan with such a sense of familial warmth. As our cautious hope grew, our ever-growing knowledge of the foster care system dampened our spirits only a bit. Our lawyer began writing up plans that went with each possible scenario. The unknown was nearly maddening.

To keep myself busy, I gathered every piece of information I could find about children from the foster care system. I learned as much as I could about cocaine and marijuana exposure. I talked with all the family members I knew and kept records of everything I learned. I began gathering all the known medical information. I knew the baby was drug exposed, but every professional we contacted assured us that there was really no long-term risk involved. We knew the baby might be born premature. She might have a higher risk of stillbirth. She may have learning delays. We discussed each new piece of information in the evenings when my husband returned from work. I felt that we could handle anything. Foolishly I believed I could wish the baby into health. I would love her unconditionally, and I believed that love would always be enough.

As it would turn out, the undetermined future was a lot less frightening than the reality we were about to face. On April 4, 2004, the phone rang again. I had just returned home from church, ready to do the last bit of packing. We had planned one final vacation as a family of three. The vacation fell at just the right time for us to take a break from the waiting game. As I walked through the front door toting my daughter, I happily called out to my husband, "Are you ready to go to the beach?" He rounded the corner with the phone still in his hand. His face was colorless and blank. "What is it?" I asked nervously.

"Um, Kristin, I don't know how to say this." He glanced down at his feet. I placed our daughter on the carpet and began removing her shoes. I didn't want to hear his words. I resisted the urge to open the front door and run. "The baby was born this morning. She was early. There wasn't anything they could do. She didn't make it." My breath caught and the room started spinning. "No." I whispered. The shoe slipped out of my hand as I stood and walked out of the room.

"We have to get to the airport. We're going to be late." I could hear the words tumble out, but they felt hollow. I mindlessly walked to my bedroom and grabbed the suitcase. Mechanically, I opened drawers and placed each item inside the bag. My fingers brushed the bassinet. Out of habit, I placed my hand on the quilt that lay inside. I began to pray for the unborn daughter. I froze, my heart constricting with the realization of my mistake. My chest felt so heavy I thought I might crush beneath the burden. One tear fell and then another. I fell to my knees, hands grasping at the emptiness around me. With each heaving breath, sadness spilled from me. "No, no, no, no, nooooo." My hand rested on the eyelet hem of her bed. The fabric felt as cold and empty as my heart. When I had no tears left, I rose again, zipped the suitcase, and left for the airport. I wouldn't talk of her again for days.

I spent a perfectly miserable four days on the beach before I was forced to talk about the baby. Mike recognized my need for space and didn't push. Finally, he pulled a beach towel up to mine and sat down next to me. Our daughter slept peacefully beside us, shaded from the sun, unaware of the conversation that was about to take place. He linked fingers with mine, and for a while we sat silently. Waves lapped at the shore. I breathed deeply the smell of salt water in the breeze.

With eyes closed I allowed myself to hear him. "I've been asked to officiate the funeral. They don't know anyone else?" It wasn't a statement, more of a question. I left it unanswered while I envisioned what that meant. I hadn't allowed myself to even think of her burial until that moment. Always the pastor's family first, we would be there to offer comfort, not receive it. "Of course," I said flatly, "it makes sense. Let them know we'll be there."

The day of the funeral was bitter cold, one of those leftover winter days that creeps unwelcomed into spring. I dressed in black and pinned my hair in loops low on my neck. I shrugged my daughter's tiny arms into her coat and pulled her braids neatly beneath her hood. We made the trip in silence and arrived faster than I would have liked. Mike shook hands and stood bravely to say kind words. I passed out tissues and tried not to think about the lifeless body at the front of the room. As the funeral began, her mother took the seat closest to the casket and motioned in my direction to do the same. I looked behind me before realizing she wanted me to sit beside her. I did, and placed my little girl on my lap. I wrapped my arms tightly around my daughter as I felt the weight of this other mother's loss. She held no one. Her children were gone, all of them — the youngest tiny child present in body but absent in soul. I placed my hand on her knee and she placed her hand on mine. When it was time to close the casket, we said our goodbyes. I stood for a moment in front of the baby, pondering the perfectly formed lips. The tiny nose, nostrils forming a flawless figure 8, just like her big sister, just like her big brother, just like her momma. Dainty eyelashes curled up toward heaven. My breath caught and I turned away.

The wind bit at us as we stood over the miniature gravesite. She would be buried among other children in a patch of cemetery called the Children's Garden. I wrapped my daughter's fingers in mine to keep them warm. *She'll be cold in that ground,* I thought. I couldn't stop thinking that. *She's going to be cold. She's going to be alone. They didn't put enough blankets on her.* My irrational thoughts never met my lips, just lurked beneath the surface, biting at my mind. I can't remember how I got back to the car or who buckled our daughter into her car seat. I traced that figure 8 onto the foggy window as we drove away. That perfect figure 8, also the symbol for infinity. The tie from mother to daughter and from one generation to the next. Broken.

Just as we approached the exit of the cemetery, I grabbed the door handle and pulled. My feet hit the frozen grass and I started running. My steps were wobbly at first, one high-healed shoe slipped off and then another. I darted through grave stones. In and out. Ragged breaths giving way to heaving wails. *I want to quit. This hurts too much. I don't want to do this anymore. Why, God? Why her? Why us?* My breaths slowed as my mind cleared. I had a beautiful daughter waiting for me in the car. The little boy and his sister were waiting for me too. With their precious faces fixed in my mind, I realized I couldn't quit now. My toes were turning numb as I walked briskly back to the car where Mike and Joelle were waiting patiently for me to come to my senses. I had begun to think clearly and had a renewed sense of purpose.

# CHAPTER 3

# Missed Birthday

Another month passed and I missed the little boy's birthday. I spent the day dreaming of him. I wondered what he was doing. I tried to picture him a little bigger, a little chubbier. Did his cheeks finally fill out? Did he miss his mom and his big sister? I talked to his mom on that day. She confessed that she had missed a visit the day before. She told me she didn't have bus fare. The excuse felt lame and without conviction. I wondered what it had been like for the little boy to know she was absent. Did he realize it was his birthday? Did he know she wasn't there? My tone was flat as I told her goodbye.

*The little boy learned to walk at ten months old. His foster mom witnessed the event. She was the mother of many, the grandmother of many more, and the foster mother of hundreds. She captured the moment on her instamatic. She carefully documented the little boy's likes and dislikes. She made careful records of his doctor's visits and waited patiently to hear his first words. The day before the little boy's birthday, she buckled him safely into his car seat and drove the hour-long drive to the visitation center.*

*They checked in 15 minutes early and shuffled to the waiting room. Her bones were aching and she wondered how much longer she could care for these tiny children. She hoisted him onto her lap and wiped his face with a baby wipe. The little boy's big sister came tumbling into the room with a brood of foster sisters and their foster mom. The little girls chattered happily as they went straight for the toy bin. Not the big sister. Her eyes remained wide with an uncertainty hidden behind them. The two foster mothers struck up their weekly conversation while the little boy wiggled off the lap and began to explore the room. The big sister followed closely behind him. Protectively she placed her arms out when he lost balance. Knowingly, she put smaller toys out of reach on an end table. At three and a half she hovered over her charge like a tiny little mother.*

*The two families waited the obligatory 30 minutes before the supervisor released them to go home. The little boy reached his arms toward his foster mom and allowed himself to be carried out of the room. The big sister stood frozen with her lower jaw jutted out. She refused to budge. Eventually her foster mother gathered the other little girls, scooped up the big sister, and turned her flailing body away from her own as she navigated the three flights of stairs down to the parking lot.*

I cried at the thought of the children waiting alone at the visitation center. I cried for their loss, their hurt, and their worry.

We continued to work toward our license and moved at a speed that we would find out later was unheard of. In June, our license was complete. I gripped the piece of paper as if my life depended on it. We had spent the past month trying to get Child Services to even speak with us. The children's mother was insisting that we be allowed to take them, but she was losing her credibility quickly among her caseworkers.

Finally, one day I appealed to my sister. She said, "Okay, let me give it a try." She called the caseworker and simply stated, "Hello, this is Rebecca from Franklin County, I'm calling about the Marks children. Please get back to me at your earliest convenience." That was all it took, a little bit of authority and a lot of self-confidence. The caseworker called back the next day. My sister gave them our phone number and told the caseworker that we were friends of the birth family and we were willing to keep the siblings together for as long as it would take. Those were the magic words, and the wheels started turning.

## The First Day Together

Within two weeks, we were connected with the little boy's foster mother. She was so happy to hear from us and set up an appointment to meet in two days. I couldn't believe that this was finally happening. I hung up the phone and called the big sister's foster mother. She got choked up on the phone and asked if it would be okay to wait one more day so that the girls could have a little going-away party. I was anxious to get my own new life started, but both conversations were humbling. I was not the only one whose life was about to be changed. Each and every one of us was about to experience loss and gain, certainty and uncertainty.

Mike was out of town the day I went to get the little boy. I buckled Joelle and two extra car seats into the car. A teenager from our church named Rachel was living with us at the time and she jumped at the chance to go along on the adventure. We chatted happily for the first 45 minutes of the drive. As we wound around country roads, passing the newly planted cornfields, the car got quieter. Even my daughter sensed the nervous silence that had begun to fill the car. I glanced at her in the rearview mirror. She had her pacifier between her teeth and was watching thoughtfully as the clouds, cornfields, and soybeans rolled by.

My hands began to sweat as I smoothed my handwritten directions along the top of the steering wheel. Old grain bins stood abandoned directly at the edge of town. Everything about this tired, Indiana town looked just as I had expected. I took a left at the single blinking light. One more block and I turned right. My stomach was a lump in my throat and my hands began to shake. We had worked for months to get to this moment, and I had begun to lose my nerve. "Look! It's right there!" Rachel exclaimed. I could see the house just as she had described it. A forest green minivan was parked a little to the left of the driveway. Two wheels touched the grass as if making way for my arrival. I parked carefully behind the rusted bumper. The three of us walked up to the door together.

The woman who answered was in her early 60s. She welcomed us into her cramped kitchen like we were old friends. Sitting in the high chair with the curliest head of hair I've ever seen, was the little boy I'd dreamed of. I passed Joelle to Rachel and crouched to eye level with the little boy. I smiled. "Meet Alexander," his foster mother said sweetly. "Hi Alexander," I returned. She began to explain all of her documents to me. She had pages and pages of observations and details written into a spiral notebook. When she finished, my head was spinning. She slipped the notebook inside of a bright red folder. On the cover, written in blue ink was "Alexander."

His foster mother produced two grocery sacks filled with his clothes and a small drawstring bag that contained all he had brought with him into care. I opened the bag to find a baby bottle crusted with Kool-Aid and a pair of footed pajamas with the toes long since worn through. My naivety shown then. "This is all he came with? Did his mom bring him anything else when she came to the visits?"

She shook her head, "This really isn't unusual. I've been a foster mom for decades. He came to me better than most." I forced myself to smile and thanked her for keeping everything for him. Alexander was wiggling in the high chair, searching for an escape route. "Go ahead." She motioned to me. I unbuckled him and lifted his tiny body effortlessly to the floor. He and Joelle played quietly for a few minutes observing one another.

Rachel and I gathered his things and carried them to the car. It only took one trip. I was becoming afraid to take him from such a happy home and found myself shuffling back to the front door. I talked to his foster mom for a few more minutes when she asked, "Are you going to adopt him?" The question caught me by surprise and I actually choked. She grabbed me a cup of water and as I regained control, I answered, "I'm just going to keep the kids until their mother gets all of this worked out."

She actually looked sad for me. "Of course, of course. Reunification is always what we hope for." Her voice trailed off and I could tell she knew more. I didn't dare to ask what her undertone meant.

"Are you sure I should be taking him from you?" I couldn't believe I had said the words that were plaguing my mind.

"Oh, honey, I'm getting to be an old lady. I only take the little ones and I only take them until they find exactly the right home. I can tell you are the right person for Alexander." I wiped away a tear and hugged her. Rachel gathered Joelle, and I gingerly picked Alexander up. We said our last goodbyes, and as the door closed, Alexander screamed.

He continued to scream while we buckled him. He wailed as we pulled out of the neighborhood. He sniffled as we passed the corn and soybeans. He began to calm as we pulled into the McDonalds parking lot conveniently situated at the halfway point between our two homes. He gave a small smile as I fed him small bites of chicken nuggets. Joelle handed him a French fry and then squeezed his tiny hand. Rachel and I exhaled for the first time in over an hour. Just then we saw a rainbow-colored hot air balloon floating just above the car. We decided to follow it. We trailed along behind the balloon for miles. Joelle squealed as we got closer and closer. As it finally began to dip toward the earth, we parked alongside a ditch and opened the sliding van door to allow the kids to get a better look. They waved and smiled while the balloon landed with a swoosh. For a few minutes we all smiled. We traveled the rest of the way home with a peaceful happiness.

Our first night at home was exhausting. Joelle clung to me as I kissed her goodnight. Alexander proved to have more energy than I thought possible. He raced through the house exploring each corner with distracted curiosity. When it was time to put him in his bed, he clawed at my face with frantic fear. I prayed over him and kissed him goodnight, but before I made it to the top of the stairs I heard a thud. He had worked his way completely out of the crib. I opened the door to survey the scene. He was flat on his back looking frustrated. "Oh no, buddy, what happened?" I said softly. I scooped him up and placed him back in his crib. We repeated this dance a handful of times before I decide to pull the rocking chair up next to the crib and try something else. For a while he resisted the rocking. He grabbed fistfuls of my hair, and each time I moved his arms back to his side, he snarled at me in frustration. His eyes darted around the room wildly. We rocked for over an hour before his body became tired and limp. I didn't dare move. I continued rocking long after he fell asleep.

When I finally placed him in the crib, I tiptoed down the stairs trying to avoid the creaky stair. Rachel and her friends were in the middle of a Harry Potter marathon. "I'm going to sleep on the floor next to the crib. Will you keep your ear out for Joelle?" I whispered.

"Sure, of course. How is he doing?" she asked.

"I'm not sure. This is so much harder than I thought it would be," I continued to whisper. She nodded and I returned to the tiny attic room with a blanket and a pillow. I spent most of the night starting at the slowly moving ceiling fan. How could helping another person feel so sad? I would have to repeat this experience again tomorrow. The last words on my lips were a prayer for the big sister who was about to come home to a place she'd never known and once again lose a part of herself.

CHAPTER 4

# Garbage Bags

My mom arrived early the next morning. I had just fixed a cup of coffee and had barely taken a sip when I heard the knock at the door. "Mom, you must have left home at 6:00 a.m.! You have no idea how glad I am to have you here." I threw my arms around her and squeezed. She followed me to the kitchen where I grabbed a second empty cup. As I poured the steaming brew, she grabbed the creamer. I introduced her to Alexander, who had already been strapped securely into his high chair. She said, "Hello Alexander," in her soft voice, which immediately prompted a tiny smile. I was impressed. Joelle of course lifted her arms to her grandma immediately. My mom sat down in between the two of them and began filling sippy cups and cutting small pieces of toast for Alexander. Without batting an eye, she expertly moved her still hot coffee out of the reach of his tiny fingers. I knew it would be so good to have her here. She would be like my right hand for the next few days and I immediately felt calm.

Our appointment to meet the little girl's foster mom was at noon, which left us plenty of time to finish breakfast and play before heading out the door. My mom and I grabbed our own bowls of cereal and sat down next to the two toddlers. I got up for a moment to top off my coffee, and when I turned around to grab my mother's cup, I was just a moment too late to stop Alexander from dumping his entire breakfast onto the floor. "Alexander!" Not fast enough. "Joelle! Absolutely not — do not throw that on the floo . . . ." Too late, she looked me straight in the eye and dropped her breakfast and her sippy cup beneath the table. Joelle and Alexander looked at each other and grinned ear to ear.

I sighed as my mom and I began cleaning up the mess. "I was worried they wouldn't get along," I exclaimed.

"Well, I guess they just proved you wrong." She responded. It was hard to stay mad, so we wiped them up quickly and released them from the confines of their respective chairs. They toddled off to the playroom and we followed quickly behind. Soon we realized time had gotten away from us and quickly changed their diapers in preparation for another car ride. As I slipped Joelle's feet into her tiny sandals, I could see my mom struggling with Alexander. He was beginning a full-on protest against shoes. It took two of us to wrestle him into footwear. We each scooped up a child and hurried out to the car.

Despite a few setbacks, we were still making pretty good time. I checked the address on a crumpled up paper I had stuffed in my pocket. We were meeting in a parking lot halfway between the foster mom's house and mine. I was thankful for the extra set of eyes as we left the empty streets of the suburbs and entered the increasingly crowded city. Store fronts gave way to empty buildings. We bumped across the abandoned railroad tracks. They actually run for a few weeks each year bringing families to the state fair. I've always wanted to ride the train, and I began to wonder if our new little family would be able to attend the fair that year. My mind jolted back to the present and I recognized a few of the landmarks. The empty parking lot stood stark in the distance. I could see nothing to indicate its former purpose except a worn sign that read, "Lawn and Garden." I pulled into the empty lot at the same time as another grey minivan. It occurred to me only then the strangeness of exchanging a child in a parking lot. Shouldn't there be some kind of official plan?

I pulled up next to the other van and rolled down my window. "Katie?" I asked.

"Yes, that's me." She carefully opened her door and I did as well. We stood and talked for just a second before she led me around to the back. She opened the hatch and immediately began apologizing. "I'm sorry. I only had one tote for her things. I had to put the rest in trash bags. I hate to do that; it just feels wrong." I nodded but couldn't respond. A knot was building in my throat. My naivety was shattered again in that moment. All this little girl had in the world was stuffed into two trash bags and a tote. I began hauling the bags to my car as Katie followed, explaining that she had picked up some extra things at her church clothing pantry. I kept nodding as she opened the side door to her van and called a very reluctant child to the front. "Camille, come on. This lady is going to take you home. You'll like it there."

Camille stepped out of the van and looked me in the eye. Then she looked at Katie. She turned without expression and walked to my van. My head began to spin. I followed closely behind her. She reached her tiny hand up and pulled herself into the van. That's when she saw Alexander. She froze, eyes locked on him. I watched as her body relaxed and she placed her hand on his knee. With her lips still pressed firmly together, she gave a small smile. He grinned up at her and relief washed over me. I hadn't realized that Katie was standing beside me. She put her arm around me. "It's good to see them back together," she said as she wiped away a tear. Camille slid into the empty car seat, and I climbed back to buckle her. Her beautiful yellow sun dress mocked the sadness in her eyes. I buckled her and spread the cheery folds across her knees. She never looked at me; she just sat with eyes fixed on her baby brother. Katie pressed her hand to the window and wished us all the best. Camille glanced her way but said nothing. The car was silent all the way home. Even the little ones sensed the sadness. Each time we stopped, I checked the rearview mirror only to find Camille still staring at Alexander.

We all watched in silence as the city slipped away. It felt as though the identity of our children fell away with it. Questions swirled in my mind. Was I doing the right thing? If I was, why did it feel so bad? The realization that I was not their savior hit as we wound around the back roads toward home. The children were not happy to live with me. They were more secure together than they had been alone, but not happy. They didn't know if I would be a safe place. I had no way to explain what had just happened. I felt like just another trauma in a long line of traumatic experiences. The crunch of the gravel driveway brought me back to my senses. I looked up at the mirror one more time to find that Camille still hadn't removed her gaze from Alexander. I wondered if she was afraid she might lose him again. I quickly unbuckled Camille, then Joelle, and finally Alexander. The three of them walked cautiously toward the door.

## Tantrums and Bubble Baths

Alexander stepped through the front door and threw his shoes off immediately. Barefoot once again, he began to run through the house, tugging his sister along with him. He pointed to each item but still hadn't uttered a word. With soft grunts he motioned her toward the kitchen, the playroom, and finally squealed and grabbed the handle to the back door. I had never seen a 13-month-old with the ability to unlock a door. His dexterity was almost as impressive as his determination. My mom and I took the kids into the backyard together. They played for hours on the swing set, stopping only to bounce a ball back and forth between them. As time passed, Camille began to relax. When our black lab bounded out the backdoor, Camille jumped and then smiled briefly before turning back to her baby brother. Joelle stepped between the dog and her new friends. She smiled at all of them, encouraging them to hug and pet the puppy. All three children found a connection and a peace while interacting with the dog. Alexander hadn't stopped moving all day until that moment. I could see his movements taper and his breathing slow as he wrapped his arms around the dog. I savored that moment of peace. Little did I know, there would be very few moments of peace in our life with Alexander.

He unfolded his arms from the dog's neck and then patted her one more time with his tiny outstretched hand. Like a flash, he was off again. He touched every plant in the back yard, climbed the fence and toppled down on his bottom. He spun in circles and then licked the patio. I grabbed him as he swung by one arm from the side of the swing set. I folded him into my arms instinctively, protectively, then he wriggled free. His eyes were wild and wide. He couldn't see everything fast enough. His little body bumped and jumped across the yard and back over and over again. He lay flat in the grass with his arms and legs outstretched, his fingers digging into the warm earth. He snarled as a blade of grass brushed past his cheek and then plucked it from the ground. Smashing the roots of the tiny plant between his palms he furrowed his brows. His presence gave off a mixture of anger and fascination.

When it was time to come in for dinner, my mom and I coaxed the girls inside. Alexander wouldn't budge. My mom took each girl by the hand and led them inside to the sink to wash up. Alexander looked at the girls and back to the yard, then stood firm. I looked to my mom for help, but she shrugged her shoulders. I scooped him into my arms and turned toward the door. The girls were inside with my mom. Their hands were poised over the sink, and they had an impossible amount of hand soap on each tiny hand. Joelle and Grandma were singing, "Rub and scrub, rub and scrub, get your hands clean." Camille was washing each tiny finger with marked concentration. Alexander was rigid in my arms. The look on his face was one of unmistakable frustration. I scurried inside with him as I heard a low growl begin in his chest.

I coaxed with my most upbeat voice, "Don't worry, Alexander. We are just going to wash our hands. See the girls are inside already. We're going to have dinner, then take a bath. It will be good, you'll see."

My words weren't having the desired effect, so I took him to the sink and squeezed a small drop of soap onto his clenched fist. He screamed. I peeled his fingers apart and pressed soap between them.

He screamed louder. I checked the temperature of the water and waved his fists under the stream. I didn't think it was possible, but he screamed even louder. I grabbed the towel and quickly dried him off. My mom and I exchanged a quick glance and then I looked at Camille and Joelle. They were buckled into their high chairs already, but their mouths hung open with a look of surprise. My heart was pounding but I was determined to keep the mood light.

My mom spoke first, "Well, everyone, it looks like we're having spaghetti tonight. I'll start fixing the plates. This looks yummy." I was so relieved to hear her cheerful voice. I buckled the flailing toddler into his seat and grabbed a plate. Just as quickly as the tantrum had started, it was over. The five of us ate around the tiny table and before the meal was over, there was a thick layer of spaghetti and sauce on every last inch of the kitchen. It was a mess but it made me happy to see them happy. At least the meal had been a success.

The combination of spaghetti, mud, grass, tears, and snot led naturally to bath time. I ran a warm bath and at the last minute decided to squeeze some Mr. Bubble into the tub. My mom graciously chose to clean the pasta disaster from the kitchen floor, and for that I am ever grateful. I corralled the three into the bathroom and began to undress Camille. She looked at the bubbles with a surprised expression. I dipped my hand into the tub to show her, and she touched the handful of bubbles tentatively. I lifted her into the tub and began to undress Joelle.

Just then, Alexander turned the handle and bolted out the door. I hadn't anticipated that move and stood up quickly. My foot slipped and I caught myself on the edge of the tub. Breathing a sigh of relief, I left the door open wide as I chased after the one-year-old. My mom heard the commotion and ducked into the bathroom to watch the girls. I caught Alexander at the bottom of the stairs and scolded him softly. He giggled and we returned to the bath. He slipped into the tub with wonder and fascination. All three children began lathering the bubbles on their arms, toes, and faces. Camille showed the other two how to make a bubble beard and they all laughed. We allowed the tub to drain while my mom and I wrapped them in warm towels.

Joelle and Camille snuggled into their jammies and Alexander began another night of fierce resistance to his bed. Once all three were finally asleep, my mom and I met on the front porch. We sat there exhausted, hands wrapped around mugs of decaf, each knowing there were no words that would begin to describe the emotions of this day.

# CHAPTER 5

# Daddies Are Scary

Mike arrived home a day later, just in time for our annual 4th of July celebration. He was thrilled to meet our newest family members. We were waiting on the front porch when he pulled into the driveway. Joelle wiggled free from my grip and scooted down the stairs. She flew into her Daddy's arms. My mom and I waited with Alexander and Camille. I couldn't wait to hug my husband. With Alexander's arms wrapped tightly around my neck, I stepped toward him and leaned in for a long-awaited kiss. Alexander reeled back and clutched my hair. Mike gave me a quick peck on the cheek and leaned toward Alexander, "Hello, it's so nice to meet you," he whispered. Alexander looked away. Mike crouched down next to Camille and smiled. "I'm very happy to see you, Camille." She too looked away and my heart broke. Mike stood up and hugged my mom. He isn't too easily discouraged but I could see the disappointment on his face.

I tried to encourage him. "It will take a while, I think. I have so much to tell you. This has been crazy." We helped him carry his bags inside and settled into the first day of our new life together.

That night as we were tucking the kids in bed, Joelle kept popping out of her bed and scampering into the hallway. We could hear the patter of her little feet as she trotted through the loft toward her waiting parents on the stairs. She would sing, "Mommy, Daddy, I'm out of bed. Come get me." Mike and I took turns scooping her up and placing her back into her bed. She giggled with sheer delight as she played her game of cat and mouse. We were so happy to be back together as a family that we avoided the strict bedtime routine as much as she did. Alexander had gone to bed quietly and Camille was tucked into her tiny toddler bed. She didn't move an inch and her eyes followed us as we played with Joelle. She made no attempt to join the fun. We finally got serious with Joelle and placed her back in her bed one more time. We kissed her forehead and smoothed her hair.

Then Mike turned around grabbed me by the waist and threw me over his shoulder. Mike, Joelle, and I burst into laughter and then we noticed Camille. She was cowering in the corner of her bed with her hands thrown reflexively over her head. She didn't make a sound, but tears streamed silently down her cheeks. "Oh no, honey, we're just having fun. No one is hurt." We moved slowly toward her. Mike sat on the floor next to her bed and I sat near her feet, "We're okay, it's just a game. I'm so sorry we scared you." We prayed with her but kept ourselves at a distance. We smiled at each of the girls before closing the door. We felt like failures.

Alexander didn't sleep through the night. Mike and I found ourselves up and down the stairs to his room more times than we could count. Finally, around 3:00 a.m., I grabbed my pillow and a blanket and settled in beside Alexander's bed. His screams turned to sobs and then just tears. I wiggled my arm through the rungs of his crib. The tightness of sorrow gripped my chest as he grasped my pinky with his tiny little fingers. That night I cried too. I pictured Alexander's momma, far away. I thought about my own mom just one room over, supporting me and loving me, and I wept at the thought of losing her. I thought about my daughter, knowing I would wake up to see her smiling face, and my heart ached at the thought of being separate from her. I couldn't imagine what these children must be feeling. I had no solution. I had no words. I found myself in the middle of a storm with no calm in sight. That night I prayed again for my family and for the little boy's family. I prayed for peace, and before the sun rose that morning I fell asleep in the arms of a Savior who I knew would not let any of us go.

Each day was a little less traumatic than the last. Each day our family grew to understand one another. We rose every day to a little more peace, a little more rest, and a little more familiarity. We began to resemble a family instead of five strangers playing roommate. Before the end of the summer we had begun to find our groove. I purchased a triple stroller at a church garage sale toward the end of July. I had wandered in on a rare day without the kids and found that they were selling everything half off their original asking price. The total came to $12 and I had enough left over to buy a gigantic doll house for $7. As I completed the sale, I impulsively hugged the sweet little church lady. She looked surprised but hugged me back. She had no idea how grateful I was for the newfound freedom the stroller would bring.

As the summer turned to fall, Mike slowly gained the trust of Camille and Alexander. We fell into the routine of pushing the stroller to the park following dinner each night. We would let the kids play until it was nearly time for bed and then wind down with a bath and a book. One night as we pushed the stroller down the gravel driveway, Camille reached her arms toward Mike and allowed him to lift her up. I unbuckled the other two, never taking my eyes off of the sight. Mike was completely focused on the precious moment and I couldn't help but let a tear fall. Joelle, always sensitive to others, reached up and wiped it from my cheek. For Camille, not all daddies were scary anymore. She had a daddy she was beginning to trust.

## Mommies Can't Be Trusted Either

Alexander was never more than an arm's reach from me the entire summer. On one hand, it was endearing. On the other, it felt desperate. He began to feel comfortable around the home and would wander from the playroom to his bedroom, making messes along the way. Alexander had a way with messes. He would dump baskets of laundry, tip over chairs, pull pots and pans out of the cabinets, drag bath towels through the house. There was simply no amount of child-proofing that would create a clean environment. He kept me on my toes during every waking moment. When we left the house, however, it was a different story. Alexander would not allow me out of his sight. A trip to the grocery store meant pushing the cart loaded up with two little girls and enough groceries for five, using only one arm. My other arm was constantly occupied with a bundle of clinging one-year-old. If I tried to place Alexander in the cart he would wriggle his feet out of the leg holes and grip the seat belt in a panic. Red bruises rose where he beat his legs against the side of the cart. I feared for his safety and for my own reputation. I didn't want marks left on his legs. I resigned myself to carrying him everywhere.

Instinctually, I knew that Alexander needed to feel safe, but the constant carrying was beginning to feel stressful. My arms hurt and I felt like I was neglecting the girls. Alexander was too big for an infant front carrier. I tried a backpack intended for hiking, but even on the flat streets of Indianapolis I felt like the weight would tip my small frame. One day on a trip to the zoo, Alexander wiggled himself free from the triple stroller no less than ten times. I stopped on a park bench and faced the stroller toward myself. With Alexander on my lap, I fished out the small baggies of snacks I had packed. I handed each child a sippy cup and got myself a bottle of water. I felt so exhausted, I wanted to go home, but the walk to the entrance seemed insurmountable. I started to cry and quickly wiped away the tears. The children were all smiles, not sensing my frustration. That's when I saw a woman walk by with the best invention. She had her toddler tied to her back with some sort of scarf. It was simple, almost primitive. I jumped up and nearly scared her. I asked her all about her wrap and she directed me toward a website that would teach me how to measure and make my own. I kissed Alexander, coaxed him back into the stroller, and headed to the car with a renewed sense of hope.

That night when the kids were settled into bed I scoured the Internet for instructions on how to make and tie a wrap. I was fascinated with all the styles and versatility. Women had been carrying their children this way since the beginning of time. I couldn't believe that I'd never seen something so simple and natural before. I had enough time to run to the store that night and purchase the fabric. I stayed up late hemming the edges with my out-of-date sewing machine. I was frustrated but grateful for the clunky old machine. I crawled into bed that night feeling excited to try it out the next day.

Alexander never did let me sleep through the night. I didn't rest long before I found myself back on the floor next to his crib. With my arm once again draped over his chest, I fell into a restless sleep. It occurred to me near morning that finding a more permanent way to sleep near my little boy would have to be found. When the house began to stir, I had barely drifted off. My body had begun to function on an amount of sleep I had previously thought impossible.

Alexander woke up with his usual exuberance. I quickly dressed him and headed to the kitchen to make breakfast before the girls woke up. He was into everything, then I remembered the wrap. I clicked open the computer and logged into the instructions. It was a little complicated to get his body into the wrap but slowly I wound the fabric around each of his newly chubby legs and across his back. He was surprisingly tolerant. With him pressed so close to my body, I could feel his heart racing. As I tightened the wrap, his heart rate slowed. He laid his head against my chest and actually relaxed. I finished up breakfast in a state of shock. This little boy was quite different from the one I had grown to know over the last few months.

That night we moved our bed into Alexander's room. It was a tiny attic room and I could touch his crib from my side of the bed. The first night he scaled the side of his crib and tumbled into my bed. He clawed fiercely at my face. Finally, he fell asleep with his fists clenching handfuls of my hair. Each night he slept a little more soundly. He moved from our bed back to the crib and we both began to rest in our new relationship.

I began to use the wrap anytime we went someplace crowded. If I sensed Alexander becoming overloaded, I would quickly wrap him up. He began to know his own need as well and would point to the wrap calling it his "pocket." I could scoop him up and place him there until he felt safe to return to the world. We began to refer to him as "our little joey." Just like a kangaroo in his mother's pocket, Alexander found safety in the closeness. With our new sense of understanding, mommies became a little more trusted too.

# CHAPTER 6

# Cat Scratch

Have you ever been scratched by a house cat? I have. I was sitting in the sunroom of my parent's house one sunny day. The cat kept her distance from me. I was never her favorite. My family rescued her after I had already left for college. The stray had been lingering outside our house for months and in a weak moment, someone finally let her inside. My mom and my sister loved the cat, which they named Francesca. I found that fitting. She was beautiful and not just a little prissy. I pretended to never care for that cat, but I secretly wanted her to love me.

One warm day, I lay with my head propped up on a pillow, book in hand, enjoying the sound of Francesca's soft purring. She lay sprawled out in a patch of sun a few feet away. After some time, she ventured onto my piece of furniture and I cautiously began petting her. She arched her back and tilted her head toward me. We were both at peace, until my rambunctious puppy came bounding around the corner. Francesca firmly planted her back claws into my leg and scrambled up my chest and leapt from my shoulder. I ran to the bathroom and quickly undressed to assess the damage. I doused myself in peroxide as I thought about what had just happened. I knew she had hurt me out of fear, but for years I winced at the memory every time I saw her.

My first encounter with my son's "cat scratch" came when he was nearly two years old. We had just spent a lovely day exploring the beach in Florida. His sweet voice filled my ears and his natural curiosity was endearing. He wrapped his arms lovingly around my neck as we picked the prettiest seashells, unearthed coquina, and watched them scurry back to the safety of the wet sand with each wave. He held the hands of his two big sisters as they ran, escaping the ocean as it rushed toward them lapping at their tiny bare feet.

We were exhausted as we buckled into our van, our hearts filled with laughter and love. We stopped at a grocery store to pick up some last-minute items for lunch. My dad and Mike went inside while my mom and I agreed to stay with the kids. My son demanded to go inside with daddy. Calmly we told him no, and I climbed into the back seat to comfort him. As I reached into his car seat, he grabbed a fist-full of my hair and bit my arm. "NO!" I exclaimed, with surprise. His entire body had gone rigid and his eyes flared, pupils fully dilated. My mom rushed to the back seat to see what was going on. He was ripping at his five-point-harness as if it were chains. Bewildered, my mom and I made eye contact. We soothed, we scolded, we held his legs, we allowed him to flail. For the next 30 minutes we could see no trace of the sweet boy we both knew. Just as abruptly as it started, it stopped. My boy was back, but damage was done. Sweaty and unnerved, I surveyed the scene. My little girls, two and three years old were shocked. With jaws dropped, they had witnessed the entire thing. My two-year-old put her pacifier back in her mouth and my three-year old closed her jaw and turned toward the window.

The men walked out to the car just as the tantrum had run its course. I could see them through the window, talking and laughing, oblivious to what was happening just steps away. I climbed over the seats and past my mom. I could not look at her face as I righted myself in my seat. The ache in my chest began to spread and my voice was quiet as I greeted the guys. Their laughing stopped abruptly as they closed the doors. Mike glanced into the rearview mirror and caught my eye. "What's going on?" He turned around in his seat and looked from my face to my mother's, to the kids.

"We're okay," I whispered. "Everything's fine. Let's just head back and fix some lunch." The car ride back bore a disconcerting silence.

Lunch continued the same way. Even the children were aware of the shift in mood. I trudged up the stairs to put the kids down for a nap. Mike followed behind, leaving my mom and dad in the kitchen cleaning up. "What happened?" he whispered as I flopped down on our bed.

"I don't know. I really don't know. He was fine. He was so good today and then it changed. He was wild. It was like his body was out of control and his brain wasn't in there." I struggled to explain the experience.

I could tell Mike was trying to understand, but neither of us had the knowledge we needed. "Did you tell him to stop? Did you try getting him out of the car seat? Maybe he was just tired." I knew he was trying to help, but I just felt more miserable. Maybe I was the problem. What kind of mother didn't know how to calm her own son? I stayed face down on the bed until Alexander woke. I glanced at the clock. It was after 5:00 and I jumped up to get the kids from bed. We shuffled down the stairs and into the kitchen where we found my mom smiling and preparing dinner. "Hi, everyone. Did you have a good nap, Alexander?" I had always known her love was unconditional but this love for my child warmed my heart. I couldn't ever remember a time I'd felt more thankful for her.

## Dry Ground and Fruitless Crops

The summer that Alexander was two was one of the hottest in Midwestern history. Each morning I would turn on the *Today Show* while I dressed the kids. All three of them were late risers, which drove my friends to jealousy. They would wake on their own and shuffle into the kitchen for breakfast. We ate together and cleaned the dishes before heading to the family room where I had their clothes, shoes, diapers, and hair accessories laid out for them. I had learned that preparation and structure were the keys to success in our daily life. I don't know why we never watched cartoons. I think it's because I don't like cartoons. All the kids seemed interested in the *Today Show* and so that is what we watched. We spent those mornings snuggling for an hour and listening to Al Roker tell us all about the weather. The weather was the same, day after day. Hot and dry. The screen would change to the local news and to the daily dialogue about corn and soy beans and still not enough rain.

Around 9:30 we would head to the local park or to the bagel shop. I'm a fierce lover of all things coffee, and I took my caffeine intake pretty seriously. If we made it around 9:30 we could get the place mostly to ourselves. Joelle had become quite the birdwatcher that summer. She had the names of many of them memorized. She carried around a tattered paperback bird book everywhere she went. The one-way glass at the nature center was a perfect place for Joelle to bird watch and for me to finish my coffee. Alexander and Camille would always grab the craft of the day from the volunteer at the desk. Alexander was constantly moving, but he always stopped long enough to do a craft. He especially loved stickers and markers. He would climb his entire body onto the craft table and stick his tongue out with deep concentration while he tried every single marker in the craft tote. Alexander would not leave one marker capped, so I decided that my volunteer contribution at the nature center was to throw out all the dried markers and match the proper caps with their counterparts. It proved to be quite satisfying for both of us.

Joelle could stay at the nature center all day, but Alexander topped out at about 30 minutes. One particularly hot day, he began to run in circles. He spun and turned until he fell firmly onto his diapered bottom. I had begun to recognize the spinning as a sign that he was dysregulated. I knew it was time to move all the kids toward the door. Joelle had a pretty strong opinion about how long she wanted to stay at the nature center. She folded her arms and turned toward the window. Alexander also had very strong feelings about continuing to spin. Camille still refused to talk and stood between the two of them with her jaw set.

I started with a soft steady voice. "Okay, kids, it's time to go for a walk. Do you want to see if we can find a cardinal?" No luck; they weren't budging. Alexander was now lying flat on the floor and Joelle was pretending not to hear me. Camille stared from me to them and back again. I often wondered if the thoughts going through her mind behind the expressionless stare had everything to do with her judgment of my inadequacy.

I tried a few other tactics and finally, crouched down next to Alexander's now flailing body and said, "Hey, buddy, do you want to find some sticks to throw into the creek?" His eyes snapped toward mine and locked into position. "Yes," he nodded. He righted himself and then reached up for my arms. As I scooped him up I felt the disappointment from the other two children who really wanted to stay. I smiled a half smile at them. "Thank you, girls. That was good listening. Let's go for a little walk and then it will be time to go home and fix lunch." Neither girl looked me in the eye. My heart felt heavy.

Not all tantrums ended that quickly. By the end of that summer we had experienced more tantrums than we could count. Sometimes I could soothe him, sometimes I could not. I had to carry him screaming and biting out of grocery stores, swimming pools, coffee shops, playgrounds, and Sunday school. That was the worst. Church was always the worst. Pastor's families are always in the spotlight and ours was no exception. We felt the cold stares of those in our congregation who couldn't understand why our child was allowed to behave like an animal. We knew what the whispers were about. I felt angry and frustrated that people who claimed to love God couldn't see my son for more than his outbursts. Mike had to continue to do his job each week. He chose to care for those who were unkind to us, but I began to hide.

My confidence withered and my shame felt as suffocating as that humid summer. I started to feel the anxiety of Sunday morning building by Friday night. I would feel almost irrational by Saturday. At first, ladies would ask me with concern why I hadn't been to Bible study. I didn't know what to say. It was too difficult to leave Alexander in the childcare and I was getting weary of the public humiliation. After a while they asked with a measured tone of condemnation. "You know how important Bible study is, right? It's especially important for our pastor's wives to set an example. I hope you'll be able to be back soon," one well-meaning, or not so well-meaning woman almost pushed me over the edge with that comment. I nodded my head and choked back tears. I was empty and dry. I would have done anything to feel the watering of my soul through the meeting together of the church. I had already experienced too much judgment to reach out for acceptance. I kept my mouth shut and didn't tell a soul how empty I felt.

That July there was a ban on fireworks, campfires, and lawn watering. We reused the bathwater each night to water our flower beds and watched everything else wither. The rainless summer had taken the joy out of everything. Fields lay barren and brown. Front lawns hadn't needed mowing in a month, and the dry blades of grass crunched beneath our feet. My family felt dry too. My heart felt parched.

Midway through August, we awoke to repeat our daily routine. We ate our cereal, we dressed, brushed teeth, and washed our faces. We walked into the family room just in time to hear the boom of thunder and see a slice of lightning just outside the window. It startled us all and we ran to the window to see thick drops of water plinking onto the dry grass. I placed my hands against the glass, looking up toward heaven. "Thank you, God," I whispered. "Thank you, God," Joelle and Alexander mimicked in unison, reaching their hands toward the sky. Camille smiled with her face turned upward. "I need You, Lord. I need You so much. Thank You for this rain. Thank You for these children. I'm sorry I don't know what I'm doing. Please show me." I prayed out loud. The Indiana ground soaked up that rain and my heart drank up the presence of the Lord in that day.

CHAPTER 7

# Her First Words

Camille didn't say a word. Camille didn't ever say a word. I heard the girls stirring around 4:00 in the afternoon. I looked at my watch and counted backward in my head. A three-hour nap was pretty good. It would make for a much easier evening with both of them. I walked to the girls' room and opened the shade. Light poured into their tiny room and filled the space. They wiggled free of their blankets. I smiled at both of them and then heard Alexander in his room. I stepped next door to change his diaper and heard the girls shuffling around their room. Joelle wasn't bothered by the lack of conversation. She chatted happily for the both of them.

"Put my socks on, Sissy. I can't do it," Joelle's request came floating down the hallway. I stuck my head back in their doorway to see Camille kneeling at Joelle's feet sliding her socks on one at a time. She gently patted Joelle's tiny foot when she was done and smiled at her. Joelle smiled back. I thought for a moment about scolding Joelle for not putting her own socks on, but I loved the way Joelle accepted Camille's role as big sister. I worried for a moment that Joelle would be crushed when they returned home, but I couldn't worry for long. A crash came from Alexander's room and I quickly returned to see him sitting naked in the middle of the floor with all of the books from his shelf scattered around. He looked pretty pleased with himself. I scooped him up and placed him on the edge of the bed to re-diaper and dress him.

Once they were all settled, we climbed down the wooden staircase. I worried that they would fall and reminded myself to fix the railing soon. We made our way to the kitchen and I poured a handful of goldfish crackers in front of each booster seat. I had learned quickly that if each child had a bowl that it was just a quick way for the crackers to end up on the floor. I poured equal parts juice and water into their sippy cups and then set the coffee maker to brew an extra pot of coffee. I was finding that I had lost a lot of sleep in the past months. Afternoon coffee was becoming a must.

"Camille wants more juice, Mommy." Joelle had taken quickly to translating her new sister's unspoken language.

"How do you know that, Honey?" I questioned.

The look on her face was matter-of-fact. "She told me." Camille hadn't uttered a single word since buckling into my car that first day. I committed to listening more carefully.

"Do you want more juice, Camille?" She looked back and nodded with one simple nod. I poured her the juice. She took it gratefully and smiled. I didn't know the key to unlocking her words but I wished deeply that I did. I prayed that I would have the patience to wait for her and the wisdom to understand her needs. With snack time over and a great nap accomplished we took off for the park.

The triple stroller was still a blessing, but as the kids grew it became increasingly difficult to push. By the time we reached the playground I was panting and desperately in need of some water. I remembered the kids' sippy cups but hadn't packed anything for myself. I unloaded them near the swings and settled in to monitoring the slide. Alexander had a tendency to go up, down, and sideways always teetering just on the edge of dangerous. Camille and Joelle loved the swings. Joelle placed her belly on the seat of the swing and pushed with her feet. Camille followed her direction and soon they were both laughing with braids and barrettes in a flurry around their faces. I left the slide for a moment and walked to the ancient water fountain just at the edge of the mulched plot. Alexander followed, chattering all the way.

I propped him on my knee and pushed the lever, ready for a cool drink. Nothing came out. We pushed again and I kept him balanced and ready but still nothing happened. Something so small could often cause him to melt down. "I don't think it's working today. I'm sorry," I said as much to myself as to him. He slid to the ground just as his sisters wandered over. "I'm sorry, girls, it's not working. I'm so thirsty too." They all looked disappointed. We stood there for a minute sweating and lamenting the water fountain when Camille pointed to the stroller and caught eyes with Joelle. "Good idea, Sissy! We have our sippy cups. Come on, let's get them." I didn't hear Camille say anything, but clearly the girls had communicated something. Alexander and I followed closely behind.

"Oh no!" shouted Joelle. She reached inside of the stroller and pulled out two empty, dripping sippy cups. She started to cry. Camille patted her shoulder and reached in for the third cup. She handed it to me first and I said, "Oh yes, look at this. What a great idea. You have sippy cups. I'm sorry the other two spilled." She gestured to me again. Motioning me to put the cup to my mouth. "No, no that's okay. This one is yours. We'll head home in a minute and get a drink there." She shook her head and pushed the cup back toward my mouth. I took a sip and smiled. All three giggled at the sight of Mommy drinking from a baby cup. We passed the cup around and took turns. Every time the cup came back to me the kids burst into fits of laughter. We laughed until our sides hurt.

The walk home seemed less long. We stopped to admire the house with the yard full of wildflowers. We waved to neighbors and passed a woman walking two rambunctious puppies. Alexander squealed at the puppies and Camille and Joelle reached out their arms toward them. "May we pet your dogs?" I asked.

"Of course. They're a little rowdy but they just love kids," she exclaimed. I stooped down to pat the smaller one on the head. The larger one shoved his nose right above his companion begging me to pet him. In the process he almost knocked me over and the kids began laughing again. "Are you babysitting or . . ." the woman trailed off.

"Oh, these are my kids," I responded, suddenly feeling a little self-conscious.

She stuttered, "I'm sorry, you just look so young. I, um, I didn't mean to offend you."

"No offense taken," I responded as I stood up and prepared to leave. I didn't want to end up in an uncomfortable situation in front of the kids.

"I was adopted too," she responded quickly.

My heart softened. "Oh, really? That's really neat. I'm from an adoptive family too. My youngest brother, my cousin, and my grandma were all adopted." We talked for a few more minutes before the puppies had placed their paws on the edge of the stroller and started licking Camille's face. She looked less than thrilled with the situation. I took that as my cue and thanked the woman for the unexpected conversation.

We strolled home to prepare dinner. Joelle unbuckled her seat belt and reached back to help Alexander with his as soon as we turned into the driveway. The gravel crunched beneath our feet and the stroller became stuck in a rut caused by years of wear. I bent down to loosen the wheel when I heard Joelle shout, "Nooooooo!" I whipped my head around just in time to see Alexander darting onto our busy road. I screamed in terror and began running and waving my arms at the cars. A woman in a minivan screeched her tires and an oversized SUV swerved just in time.

My heart pounded, blood rushing in my ears. I scooped Alexander up into my arms and waved thankfully at the drivers. I turned back to the driveway to see Joelle and Camille watching, standing very still. I burst into tears. I knew I was scaring them but I couldn't stop. My legs gave way under me and I clutched all three children close. "Please don't ever do that. Okay? Please, it's so dangerous. You can get hurt. Are you listening to me? Do you hear me? All three of you. Please don't ever do that." My tears subsided and I gripped all of them tightly. "I'm sorry Mommy was crying. I was just scared. Everything is fine now. Let's head inside and make some dinner." I walked behind them with the vigilance of a sheep herder. I locked all the doors and placed baby gates in front of them. Still shaking, I put a movie in the DVD player and settled the kids in with a blanket and fresh cups of water. I returned to the kitchen and slumped into a chair. How could I have let him run off like that? I felt desperately inadequate.

I took a deep breath with my head in my hands. It could have been such a different outcome. I pictured his little body in pieces. The faces of those driving who hadn't expected a toddler to be in the road. I could hear the screams, the sobbing. I imagined my own horror. I saw the girls' faces. What would we have done? How would I have told his mother, Mike, the caseworker? Would I have gone to jail or lost the other children because of neglect? I hadn't meant to let that happen. He was just so fast. It was the stroller, the wheel. Oh, my heart felt as if it would burst. I only looked away for a moment. It could have been a tragedy.

Finally, I wiped my puffy eyes and blew my nose. I turned my head to see three healthy, beautiful children laughing at a Disney movie. They were fine, he was fine. I blew my nose one more time and dropped to my knees. "Thank You, Lord. Thank You for these children. Thank You for giving us one more day together. I know it could have been different, but it isn't. They are fine. Your hand was on my son today and I am fully and completely aware that his life is in Your hands just as it has been since the day he was conceived. Your hand was on my daughters today. You turned Joelle's head just at the right time. Thank You for giving her a voice for me to hear. Thank You for giving me the legs to run. Thank You for focusing the drivers on what was before them. This day is Yours. This life is Yours." I rose, dusted off my knees, and fixed dinner.

The back door creaked as Mike entered. "How was your day?" he asked cheerfully. Puffy-eyed, I turned and hugged him tightly. "Oh no, what happened?"

"It's fine. Really it's fine." I choked on the words. I told the whole story while he hugged me. It was a relief to get it out of my head and see someone else's reaction. "It wasn't your fault. Alexander's a handful. You couldn't have known he was going to do that. You have to forgive yourself. Besides, look at him. He's fine." I nodded my head and released myself from his arms.

We set the table together just in time for the kids to finish their show. I wiggled Alexander into his seat and Mike kissed the girls' cheeks as he placed them in theirs. I breathed a sigh of relief even as I pushed Alexander's plate back onto the table for the tenth time. Camille dropped her own spoon and it teetered on the edge of Joelle's chair. Joelle reached her long arms between the seats and retrieved the spoon. She handed it back to her sister and that's when I heard it. "Thank you, Sissy." It was Camille. Mike and I exchanged glances. Her voice was lovely, and once again I was in tears. Trying not to embarrass the children, I ducked my head and wiped the drops with my napkin, thanking God for the second time that day for His amazing miracles.

CHAPTER 8

# Praying for a Brother

In the winter of 2007, Kate came to live with us. She lived with some friends of ours from July until November as a foster daughter. Our friends were nearing the end of their time as foster parents and had a surprise baby on the way. I first learned about Kate while I was fostering a rambunctious nine-year-old and his baby sister. Our house was buzzing with activity. We found that cramming four car seats into our minivan was a terrible amount of hassle. We intended to continue fostering even after the kids went home, so we began searching for a larger vehicle. After a few weeks of hauling all five children around to dealerships in our free time, we finally found a 12-passenger van that was in our price range. It was a little smelly, but all the seat belts worked and so did the air conditioning. We drove it proudly into our driveway the day our friends walked over with their new charge.

Kate was adorable. She had a sweet face and bleach-blonde hair. She had more makeup than necessary, but delicate features remained visible. She was shy and soft-spoken in the midst of two very active families. I wondered what she must think of all of us. She was the youngest of three children in her family, but the other two were grown, so she was the only one taken into care. She liked basketball and little kids. She took immediately to all the babies and they instantly liked her as well. For the next few months she lived with our friends, and we had many opportunities to get to know her. As our friends neared the end of their time as foster parents, it became apparent that Kate's parents were no closer to completing their services. The caseworker began looking for new families. I wondered what would happen to Kate but didn't know if there was anything we could do about it. We received the call that the nine-year-old and the baby were going to be reunited with their mom. We were overjoyed. We celebrated their reunification, but the day they went home, our house felt very lonely.

Kate still had no place to go, but I wasn't sure we were ready to parent a teenager. It felt silly to consider it in the midst of raising Camille, Joelle, and Alexander, who were still only six, five, and four years old. I couldn't get the thought of Kate out of my mind. One afternoon I picked Camille up from half-day kindergarten and put all three down for a rest. In the quiet of my little home, I sat down on the stairs and looked out the window into the tiny backyard garden we had planted after Zoe died. I pressed my forehead to the window and felt the emptiness in my heart as freshly as I did the day we lost her.

Immediately I thought of Kate again. The grief she must be feeling over her family was more than I could comprehend. I tucked my knees beneath me and allowed myself to feel the cold pane of glass between my skin and the outside world. "Father, what would You have us do? We wanted a baby and You know that. We longed to hold just one tiny child, but all I can think about is Kate. It's not the baby I was hoping for, but she is a child and she has no one. Please don't let me be selfish about this. I want to do what's right. Am I even capable of being a parent to a teenager? Is that even what You're asking me to do? Your will be done." I laid myself before my Lord and submitted to His will. I laid there for a while longer, and when I rose I knew exactly what I had to do.

I picked up the phone and dialed the number by heart. "Hey, Mike. How's work going today?"

"Um, good I guess. What's up?" I could tell he was surprised by my afternoon call to his work line.

"I can't stop thinking about Kate," I said abruptly. I hadn't told anyone what I was thinking, but it was good to say it out loud.

"Yeah, me too," he responded with a laugh.

"Do you think we're supposed to be doing something?" I asked.

"I do," he answered. "I know it sounds crazy but I've been thinking about having her live with us. I mean, if she stayed with us she could keep going to the youth group at church and she wouldn't have to change high schools. I know we aren't ready for a teenager, but I feel like the Holy Spirit keeps nudging my heart. Is that crazy?" He blurted all of that out without taking a breath.

I had to laugh. "That's exactly what I've been thinking. I was just afraid to say it to you. I know people will think we're crazy, but I'm pretty sure they already do." Then we both found ourselves laughing.

I called my friend that afternoon and was relieved to find that they had been thinking the same thing. We contacted Kate's caseworker and the move was approved. Our friends sat down with Kate first to talk about the plan then allowed us to ask her as well. We knew that no child wanted to have to move from home to home, and we were cautious even as we asked her. "We would like to invite you to come live with us if that's okay with you. We have a room for you and we can paint it any color you like." She agreed in her typical shy way and we all began making plans to transition her to our home.

We painted her room a beautiful bold shade called sunset pink the week she came to live with us. She came over and helped paint a little until we realized with some dismay that painting wasn't her strength. My friends and I agreed to finish the painting if she and her friends would stay firmly on top of the loft bed and far away from any paint supplies. They agreed, and within a day the room glowed like a summer sky after a rainstorm. The color filled my heart with joy and when I looked at her smile, I knew it made her happy too. However, it did not make Alexander happy. He paced outside the room while we put the final touches on Kate's room. "More pink, more sisters," he grumbled.

The night Kate came to live with us, we did our best to make her feel welcome. Joelle and Camille picked out a stuffed animal to place on her bed and Mike and I ordered pizza. We set the dinner table and made awkward conversation. When it came time to bless the meal I said, "Who would like to pray tonight?"

Alexander's hand shot up. "Me!" he stated firmly.

"Okay, Alexander, I appreciate your enthusiasm."

He bowed his head and squished his eyes shut tight. I stifled a laugh. "Dear God, please give me a brother. There are too many sisters here. Amen." He opened his eyes and immediately took a bite of pizza. My head shot up and I made eye contact with Kate just before everyone burst into laughter. I was relieved to see she wasn't offended.

Kate quickly fell into the routine of our family. She had never been a big sister, but loved being adored by the little kids. Camille and Joelle often snuck into her room to examine her clothes, perfume, and makeup. They were horrified by the fact that her bed was never made. "Mommy, it's not fair," Joelle whined. "I have to make my bed every day." I had to admit it wasn't fair, but after all that Kate had been through it was one thing I wasn't going to fight about. A part of me felt good that she was getting comfortable enough with us not to tiptoe around the rules all the time.

One morning as I got the little girls ready for school, Joelle disappeared. I sent Camille upstairs to find her, but she didn't return either.

I called for them, checking my watch. "The bus is going to be here soon!" I shouted. Finally, they sheepishly peered over the top of the stairs. Joelle had on bright pink lipstick and Camille smelled like the inside flap of the teen vogue magazine. "What did you do?" I gasped.

"Nothing, Mommy. We're ready for school now," Joelle looked at me with a straight face.

"Camille, do you have anything to tell me?" I questioned. She stuttered and her eyes darted back and forth for an impossibly long time. "We're you in Kate's room?" I asked again. They both shook their heads. I questioned for a while longer and finally realized the school bus was imminent and I was not going to get a truthful answer anytime soon.

I grabbed Alexander's hand and flew up the steps. I had learned a long time ago not to leave Alexander alone for long. I plopped him on the bathroom counter and called the girls in to get a better look. We were going to miss the bus for sure, so I grabbed a wash cloth and got to work. I scrubbed Joelle's face and sent Camille to get a change of clothes. "I know you like Kate, but you have to respect her space. That is her room and it's private. She had to leave a lot behind when she came here. It's really important that we don't touch her special things. Okay?" When the smelly clothes were safely in the hamper and faces were washed back to the acceptable fresh-faced look a kindergartner and first grader should have, I hugged each of them.

Alexander plopped down off the counter and grumbled again, "Too many sisters." I had to sort of agree with him this time. The bathroom was beginning to look like a feminine war zone. I squeezed his hand and loaded the kids in the car, preparing for a late arrival to school.

I called the teacher as I pulled into the parking lot. I explained what happened and we had a good laugh. "Did you take a picture?" she asked.

"Oh man, I wish I would have. It wasn't funny 30 minutes ago, but I guess it is now." I hung up, feeling relieved that my kids went to a school with such wonderful and understanding teachers.

The girls had an afterschool club that afternoon, so Alexander and I picked Kate up from school. We barreled into the parking lot in our humongous white van. I pictured Kate's humiliated face in my mind and I had to laugh a little. Getting to embarrass a teenager was one of the unexpected joys in raising an older child. Alexander and I pulled right up in front of the double doors. He unbuckled from his car seat and stood with one hand on my shoulder and the other waving wildly. I joined in and we flagged her down with silly grins on our faces. Much to my surprise, she spotted us and began waving both arms while smiling ear to ear. She jumped up and down until we reached her on the sidewalk. By then all three of us were doubled over in laughter. That night Kate shot baskets with Alexander in the driveway and we practically had to drag our son inside as the street lights came on.

Alexander played happily in a bubble bath and even brushed his teeth without being asked twice. I scooped him out of the tub and wrapped him in a warm towel, placing him on my lap to dry. "What was your favorite part of the day?" I asked.

"Basketball," he said with a swift nod of his head.

I squeezed him close. "I'm glad you had fun. See, sisters aren't all bad!"

He squirmed free from my arms and bounded into his room. As I wiggled him into his pajamas he looked at me thoughtfully, "Momma, you know how you prayed for me when I was a baby?"

I was surprised and felt my voice catch in my throat. "Yes, I started praying for you before you were even born." I tried to catch him in my arms but he turned himself upside-down trying to find the right hole to put his arm through in his pajama shirt. I wiggled his free arm into the proper place. "What made you think of that?" I inquired.

"Tonight I'm going to start praying for a brother." He climbed into bed and folded his hands.

"I think that's a wonderful idea, Alexander," I encouraged. He faithfully prayed for a brother every night for the next two years.

# CHAPTER 9

# Persistent Prayers

"Dear God, sisters aren't so bad. I like them and everything. I just want someone to burp and fart with. Amen."

My eyes snapped open and looked directly into the face of my youngest child. "Alexander!" I scolded, but not too convincingly.

Just an hour earlier Alexander had thrown a tantrum over the brand of toothpaste available. He walked into the bathroom and climbed up on his stool. He grabbed the toothpaste with one hand and his toothbrush with the other. He squeezed with all of his might and the white liquid poured on top of the bristles. As it dripped off the brush he screamed in horror, "I want the blue kind! I want the blue kind! I want it, I want it, I want it." I raced to edge of the sink trying to comprehend the emergency.

"What?" I asked, with confusion.

"I want the blue kind." His fists were clenched and his entire body was stiff.

"Stop it, please," I snapped. I grabbed his toothbrush and rinsed the excess off. I picked him up and plopped his bottom onto the edge of the sink. He scooted off and fell to the floor. He hadn't even tried to break his own fall. "That's enough." I stood him on his feet and tried again to brush his teeth for him. I squeezed his cheeks trying to get his lips to move from his front teeth. His jaw stayed clamped. I moved his lips with my fingers and wedged the brush inside. He gagged. His eyes darted around looking at anything but me. "Stop it!" I yelled. I hadn't noticed Camille and Joelle standing behind me.

Camille flew at my legs and bit me. "Aghhhhh!" I screamed. I looked down to see her wrapped around my right leg. "Stop it, both of you. Stop it right now. It's just a toothbrush. Please stop." My body felt like it had detached from itself. I saw two terrified, angry children beneath me and one more watching the entire thing unfold. I dropped the toothbrush. It hit the tile with a tiny thud. My mind registered the smear of toothpaste that was now on my toe. I reached down and peeled Camille's fingers from my ankle. I stepped over her prostrate body and turned my back to the still screaming little boy. Joelle's arms were stretched out to me, her eyes locked on mine. I scooped her into my arms. "I'm sorry, I'm sorry, I'm sorry," I whispered in her ear.

Her little arms wrapped around my neck. "I know, Momma."

I took her to her room and tucked her in while Camille and Alexander stood frozen in the bathroom still screaming. I couldn't go back. I just wanted it to stop. I checked the clock. It had been going on for 30 minutes. I heard crashing and wondered how much damage there would be this time. I just couldn't get my heart to stop racing. I knew myself well enough not to go back in until I was calm.

I took a few deep breaths and forced a smile toward Joelle. "I love you. Sweet dreams. Everything will be fine. I'm going now. They will be fine, okay?" She nodded but looked away. I rose and shuffled toward the bathroom.

Camille was standing in the corner with arms folded watching as Alexander filled the toilet with rolls of toilet paper and paper towels. He was flushing and unwrapping with a fury. The toothpaste was squeezed out entirely onto the sink and floor. A small decorative toothbrush holder lay smashed into a thousand tiny colorful pieces. Alexander was still unresponsive to eye contact. Spit dripped from his angry mouth and he had ripped the bottom of his pajama pants. "Come on, Camille." I reached my hand out to her but did not dare touch her. She looked one more time at her brother and turned toward me. She followed me to her room.

I could sense my own detachment as I forced the bedtime routine with Camille. I didn't want to feel that way toward her. I wanted to wrap my arms around her and take away whatever lingering memory had caused her to attack. I knew it wasn't on purpose. I knew the blank expression she wore was just a mask. In my gut I knew it, but in my body I wanted to run. I motioned to the bed and she crawled in without looking my direction. "I know you are sorry about biting my leg. I'm sorry for yelling. I know it's scary when Alexander throws a tantrum." She turned away from me and faced the wall. I pulled her pink blanket tightly around her and placed my hand on her shoulder as I began to pray. "Lord, please take care of Camille while she sleeps." She moved her shoulder away from me and I felt my chest tighten. "I love her no matter what. Please heal this family. Amen."

I rose from the edge of Camille's twin bed and pressed my hand on the light switch. I made my way back to the bathroom where I found Alexander removing the toilet paper from the clogged bowl and placing it in the trash can. I sighed and wished Mike would return from his church meeting. "Thanks for helping clean up," I said wearily. I reached onto the top shelf of the hall closet and fished out the cleaner. I couldn't leave the combination of toothpaste and toilet germs for long. It made my skin crawl to think about it. I sprayed the bathroom from top to bottom and began to wipe. Finally, I stripped Alexander from his sopping pajamas and washed his hands vigorously in the sink. I had no words for him. I just scrubbed. Methodically, I moved from one end of the room to the other, sending him to put on a fresh pair of clothes. To my relief, he did what he was told.

"God, I think You made a mistake. I really do. I'm not the right mom for this. I don't have the patience I need. I just don't. I'm sorry I lost my cool a little bit ago, but I feel on edge and nervous every time he opens his mouth. I just yelled at all of my kids about a toothbrush! That isn't the type of mom I want to be. I want to understand what's going on with him, but I just don't get it. I know he's been hurt, but this is more. ADHD? That doesn't seem right either. The pre-school teacher is pressuring me to get him to behave better, but I can't get through to him. It's like he's two different people. You see that, right? Of course You do. You're God. Sorry I said that. I see what's happening to Camille and Joelle too. And for that matter, Kate. She's older but she needs attention too. I feel like I spend every ounce I have on Alexander. Will he grow out of this? Everyone tells me his actions are because he's a boy. Boys are different, but this is so intense. This isn't just a little rambunctious — it's out of control. Please help me. Please. Your will be done. Amen."

I put the last paper towel into the trash can and tied the trash bag around the dripping waste. I lifted the bag and placed it inside of a second one, hoping to keep the mess from dripping all the way out to the trash. I placed the bag at the top of the stairs and turned to see Alexander standing in his doorway holding his favorite book. "Not tonight, buddy. That tantrum took up all of our reading time." He dropped the book to the floor, and for a moment I thought we were starting up again. He didn't though. He turned to his bed and climbed under the frog-printed blanket I had sewn for him years earlier.

I tucked the blanket around him and ran my fingers along the tiny stitches. The night I made the blankets, my friend and I stayed up well past midnight cutting, ironing, and sewing. We made three for my kids and two for hers. Her youngest two daughters were recently adopted, and for both of us, life was full of wondrous possibility. We were both filled with the joy of new life. When we tied the last knot, we tiptoed into the kids' rooms and replaced their old blankets with the new. Our children woke up the next morning with excitement. They thought it had happened by magic while they were sleeping. The memory of that morning flooded back to me as I knelt next to Alexander's bed to pray. My reality was so different from the fantasy I had conjured when he first came home. I felt exhausted and spent. I didn't have the words to pray that night, but he did. "Dear God, sisters aren't so bad. I like them and everything. I just want someone to burp and fart with. Amen."

Alexander knew what he wanted, but it wasn't possible. There is no way God was ever going to entrust me with another child when I couldn't figure out how to care for the four I already had. Especially my little boy. I flicked on his nightlight and closed the door behind me. I began to pick the bag of garbage from the top of the stairs, but sank to my knees instead. "God, me again. I know he wants a brother, but I'm not doing a great job here. There is nothing I desire more in my heart than to have more children. I know You know that. I trust You to plan my life. I trust You to direct me with Alexander. Amen." I descended the stairs and tossed that bag into the trashcan, closing the lid on the mess as well as the messy night.

Mike pulled into the driveway just as I turned toward the house. It was hard for me to not be angry with him. It felt like the drama always happened when he wasn't home. I turned around to see his tired face. "Rough night?" I asked.

"You have no idea," he retorted.

"You'd be surprised," I snapped back. We walked into the house and sat at the kitchen table opting to forgo the dinner leftovers and head straight to a tub of chocolate ice cream. He told me about the meeting and the petty things people were mad about in the church. His weary words hurt my soul. We had both gone into ministry to serve others and lead them to the Lord. In many ways we did, but it sometimes felt false. We poured into our church only to have members angry with us over which version of the Bible we taught from during the teens' small group or some other small detail.

"Do you think Camille and Alexander's mom would be welcome at our church?" Mike asked suddenly. He set his spoon onto the table and looked me straight in the eye.

I had to look away. "I don't think so," I said softly. Increasingly I had begun to see the discrepancy between what the churches in our area claimed to believe and what they actually did. It was common to see an advertisement, *All are welcome here!* But we knew from personal experience that sometimes we weren't even welcome. Alexander's behavior had become increasingly concerning in public and we found ourselves feeling very ashamed.

"How was your night?" Mike asked.

I explained all that had happened and then told him about Alexander's persistent prayer. "He prays every night for the same thing. He's convinced God is going to bring him a brother." We both shook our heads and had to feel proud of our little boy's faith. Now if only we could have the same faith that God would heal our son. We longed to possess that same faith that God would heal our own brokenness.

# CHAPTER 10

# Prayers Answered

In February of 2009, Mike and I traveled to Florida to celebrate my birthday. We met up with my parents and spent two days engrossed in adult conversation, dinners out, and walks on the beach. My birthday came and went, and the following day we got on a plane to fly home. We were excited to see our children. We had just experienced a failed adoption and the trip had provided us with healing and a newfound strength. Unbeknown to us, as we boarded the airplane, Sage was entering the world in central Indiana.

We returned home and gathered our four rowdy children from various friends. We hugged their faces and settled in for the typical post separation fall-out. Kate wanted to go to her boyfriend's house immediately, and when we told her no, she sighed and asked to go to her friend's house instead. "Not if your friend's name is Josh," we retorted. She didn't think we were funny and shuffled up to her room, shutting the door hard enough that we could hear it, but not enough that we could accuse her of slamming the door.

Camille felt she had been placed in charge while we were gone. Despite being eight years old, she knew the rules and routine of everyone in the house better than her own. She immediately started a lecture with her sister about shoes in the house. Then she turned to me and said, "Are you going to leave your suitcase in the family room all day?" I lost the warm fuzzy feeling of reunification I had been clinging to. Joelle rolled her eyes at her sister and attached herself to my arm while I unpacked. Alexander hugged us warmly when we walked in the door. He climbed up my side using my arm as a brace. He wrapped his arms around my neck, almost knocking me over with the weight of his six-year-old body. Before long he was pressing his head into my side and running his shoulders into the walls while we tried to reconnect.

Bedtime wasn't too bad. We tiptoed into each of their rooms and whispered goodnight one last time before we climbed into bed. "I never thought I would say this, but I think I'm finally okay with our failed adoption. I was so angry for a while but I come home to our kids and I'm just so thankful for them that it's hard to be disappointed anymore. If I'm being honest, I never thought we were supposed to adopt another baby girl anyway. I envision us with one more little boy." I rolled over to see Mike's expression.

"I agree," mumbled Mike, "we need some more boys around here."

The following day was a holiday and we were all excited for a day home from work and school. We planned to have friends over for lunch before the obligatory holiday naptime we had scheduled. They brought their baby over and the conversation quickly turned to fostering. They had been foster parents almost as long as we had. One of their long-term placements just reunified and they were feeling that deep sense of joy and loss that no one ever seems to identify or understand in foster parenting. We grieved with them. We had just been a part of the reunification of a six-month placement. We loved the little boy and girl very much but we also loved their mom and dad. It had been months and we were still pulling baby girl socks from the laundry or baby bottles from underneath the couch cushions. Ever-present reminders that someone else had lived and been loved in this home.

My friend and I were cleaning up the lunch dishes while our husbands roughhoused with the kids. They were occupied with a mean game of hide and seek when I heard my phone ring from upstairs. I usually wouldn't run to get the phone. All of my children were home and there was nothing pressing that I knew about. For some reason, I jumped at the sound and took the stairs two at a time. I reached my bedroom and snatched up the phone on the last ring. "Hello."

"Hello, this is Angie from Delaware County. I have a newborn here at the office. I was wondering if you would be interested in taking him. We think it will just be until the weekend." My breath caught and I stumbled over my words. I mentally calculated the amount of bedrooms and beds. I knew exactly where the crib was packed, and I was pretty sure I had the baby blankets tucked up on the top shelf of my closet. "Hello," she said again, questioningly.

I stuttered back, "Oh, yes I'm here. I think, well, yes. When do you need me?"

"Would you be able to pick him up within the hour?"

I thought about it for a moment. "No problem." I nodded to myself. She hung up, and I stuffed the phone in my back jeans pocket.

I took the stairs two at a time once again. I looked at my friend's questioning face. "They want me to go get a newborn. It's a boy, and his name is Sage."

Mike peaked out from his very obvious hiding place behind the pantry door. "What?" His face looked less than amused. "I thought we were done fostering."

I honestly felt shock. "I thought we were done with private adoption, not fostering. They need us. What should we do?" I stumbled over my words again. I caught a glimpse of our friends backing gracefully out of the conversation and into the other room. "I'm really sorry," I said. "I thought this was no big deal. I didn't know you didn't want us to take any more kids."

He looked at his feet and then back to me. "I don't know what else to say. I don't really want to foster anymore. I don't think we can leave a baby without a home either. Go get him. We'll work it out." I felt giddy. My friend offered to ride with me to the DCS office.

The tension let up considerably as we buckled into the car. "Did you see his face?" I asked. "Did you see my husband's face? He was shaking his head and looking directly at me the whole time I was talking. I thought his head was going to fly completely off his neck!" She started to laugh. I couldn't help it, I did too. I felt bad for misunderstanding the conversation about foster care and adoption with my husband. I clearly thought the door was open, and Mike clearly thought the door was closed. I knew we would have some things to smooth over once I returned home.

We pulled up in front of the Delaware county DCS office. The drab grey building stood camouflaged against the winter sky. I trudged through the parking lot as slush slipped into my pretty red flats. I cursed at myself for not stopping to put my winter boots on. With the empty baby seat slung over one arm, I pulled my coat tighter against the wind. The decal on the front door was the bright blue outline of a child and an adult. It caught my eye. I had been inside the office often enough to know that the loving picture did not represent the turmoil beyond those doors.

I stomped the remaining snow from my shoes as I entered the lobby. I introduced myself to the woman behind the glass. She recognized me and ushered me down a long hallway. In a tiny waiting room there stood stacks of gently used baby toys and a few packages of diapers. In the center of the room, in a bouncy seat, was the tiniest baby I'd ever seen. His skin was so white it was almost translucent. I could see the tiny veins, blue against his slightly pink forehead. He was wrapped in a purple blanket. I crouched down next to him as I waited for the caseworker to appear. I lifted the blanket looking for his tiny toes. A fluffy pink sleeper covered his tiny legs. I looked up just as the caseworker walked in. "I thought it was a boy?" I questioned.

"He is. We didn't have anything left here at the office. The nurses found this to send him home in. We all feel so bad about it. Little guy." She sounded sad. I knew her job was hard all the time, and I could only imagine it was the little things that finally got to a person.

I stood up and shook off the thought. "No problem at all," I said. "He looks pretty handsome to me." She smiled, a little relieved.

"I have tons of clothes at my house. We'll grab them when you drop me off," my friend spoke up from behind me. The caseworker filled me in on a few details, and I left only 15 minutes after arriving.

Children change hands without a second thought, like a borrowed sweater. I put my new charge in my car and drove away. Our drive home was quiet. We were both thinking of the weight this lifestyle carried. Oblivious to how his life was changing, Sage never made a sound. My friend and I carried Sage inside her home and placed him on top of the kitchen table still bundled up in his carrier. She worked quickly to gather bottles, clothes, blankets, and even a leftover container of formula. She wouldn't let me leave until we put some proper going-home clothes on him. Once he was zipped into his pale blue footed onesie he looked ready to meet his new temporary family. "It's just till the weekend," I said as we oohed and aahed over his cuteness.

"Yeah, right! That's what they always say," she shot back. I had to admit she was right. I hugged her and thanked her for everything and prepared myself for the icy drive home.

As I drove, I wondered about his mother. I wondered if her heart was hurting and her arms were aching. I pictured what she must look like. The temperature had warmed enough that the snow melted instantly as it fell. I turned the windshield wipers on and listened to their almost silent swish. Just ahead of me the clouds parted and the sun shown low in the sky. Beams of light reflected off the still-falling snow. The roads were slick, and I vowed out loud that I would keep this little boy safe for his mother. I wondered out loud how she could have let him go. I knew a little of her story and I knew she had made a lot of mistakes. I also knew she was human just like me. I prayed for her as we made our way home, and I prayed for Sage who still sat sleeping in the backseat. I prayed for my husband and children who would be waiting at home, that all of us would have peace that night.

I pushed open the front door with one hand while cradling the carrier in the other hand. A grocery bag filled with baby items was propped against my elbow. I never want to take two trips and tonight I was beginning to regret that choice. I got the door open just a crack when I tripped and lost all my belongings onto the mudroom floor. Everything except the baby. He was still firmly in my grip. The kids came tumbling into the room stepping on all the baby clothes. I wanted to yell, but their enthusiasm over the new baby warmed my heart. I set him down and went about gathering all the clothes and shutting the door to the cold outside.

The kids did not take their eyes off him the entire night. They fixed his bottles, brought him blankets, and even shared their toys. Alexander kept a strict watch at all times. If Sage coughed, cried, or even moved his pinky finger, Alexander ran to him. "Okay, brother, it's okay." Alexander had been asked to leave his Sunday school class just the week previous for pushing other students and bursts of anger toward classmates and teachers. Seeing him so gently loving this tiny baby was a direct contradiction to his bursts of rage. "I love my new brother so much," Alexander sighed.

Mike and I exchanged worried glances. I wondered how to break the news that this was only a temporary brother. Mike crouched down next to our son. "Hey buddy, I know you love Sage, and I know you want a brother very much, but the baby is only staying a little while. You remember what we've told you about being a foster family? It means we help children who need us just until their moms and dads can take care of them again. Okay?"

Alexander looked at us like we were crazy. "I know all of that. You helped me too, but I never went home. I'm sure Sage is staying too. I asked God for him." We both let out an audible breath. When Alexander was convinced of something, there was absolutely no convincing him otherwise. What we didn't know that first night was that Alexander was absolutely right. Sage was the brother he had diligently prayed for.

# CHAPTER 11

# An Abundance of Brothers

As a first grader, Alexander still did not recognize all 26 letters. Beginning readers were complicated and frustrating to our son. We tried everything to help him learn to read. One night as we curled up on the couch to work on a story he brought home from school, I noticed his body tense as we opened the book. "Honey, what's wrong?" I asked.

"Nothing!" he snapped back. I chose to ignore the uneasy feeling I had. It was getting close to bedtime, and I just wanted to wrap things up for the day.

I read the title page and then gestured for Alexander to read the first sentence. "Table, dog, ball." He snapped at me again.

"What? That doesn't make any sense. Let's try again." I pointed to the first word. "T-H-E. Remember that word? It was one of your sight words last year." I encouraged.

"Dog, ball, boy," he replied.

"Okay, let's try something else. I'll say the sentence and then you repeat after me. Okay?" I was trying to keep my voice calm, but I was already feeling the stress. "The dog runs," I said.

"The dog, ball," Alexander responded.

"Let's try again." I knew my voice wasn't hiding my frustration. With one movement, Alexander ripped the book from my hands and tore the first page in half. He jumped from the couch and ran through the kitchen while I was still untangling myself from the blanket.

When I finally caught up to him he was curled up in a ball inside a basket of shoes. He pulled intensely at his hair and clumps dislodged from his scalp. I put my hands on his arms. "Hey, kiddo, let's stop pulling hair, okay? Let's just talk about this. It's okay. I knew you were frustrated. I'm sorry. We can take a break."

He glared at something past my face. He stared so intently I almost believed something was behind me. After a few moments I turned to look, and a shiver ran down my spine. Nothing there. I knew there wouldn't be, but it was as if Alexander saw something none of the rest of us could see. I tried to move into his line of vision. I moved my head an inch to the left while placing my hands on top of his fingers. He moved his head farther. I wrapped my fingers around his and removed them from the hair. He kept a fierce grip that matched his intense stare. I continued to talk calmly, keeping my voice low. "I'm not mad at you Alexander. I love you so much. Please look at me. Please move your hands, okay? You need to stop hurting yourself. Jesus made you and you are so important to Him. Please stop."

His head whipped around and he looked me right in the eye. "I don't love you," he said.

His fingers had loosened, and I took the opportunity to remove them from his hair. "That's okay. You are mad right now. I understand. I love you, though, and Jesus does too." I kept my hands loosely on his. Before I could react, he grabbed a handful of my hair and pulled. The yelp escaped from my mouth before I even registered where the pain was coming from. "No! Alexander, no!" I tried to regain my composure, but I felt a chunk of my hair release into his tiny hand. I reached back behind my head and pulled his fingers loose. I twisted his arm back as I scooted away. I hadn't meant to hurt him but I could tell by the shocked look that I had.

His face suddenly returned to normal. His eyes had lost the hollow look from moments ago. He yelled, "You hurt me. You hurt me! I'm going to tell. I'll tell my teacher."

I rubbed the spot of missing hair as I scooted away. I was shocked by what had just happened and even more shocked by his response. The fear of being investigated was always present in my foster parent brain. I knew I was only trying to help him calm down but I began to shake at the thought that someone else might not see my actions that way. "Alexander, I'm sorry I hurt you. You were hurting me, and I needed to get your hands off me. I'm sorry I twisted your arm. Are you okay?"

He rubbed his arm. "Yes, I'm sorry I did that, Momma." My heart was racing and I tried to slow my breathing. My world had gone dark in the intense moment, and things began to come back into focus. I stayed on the mudroom floor and he stayed in the basket for a long while.

I spoke first. "Alexander, I'm not sure what happened, but if you are feeling frustrated you need to tell me. Okay? You can't hurt yourself or others. This is really important." To my surprise, he nodded and crawled into my lap. We sat on the mudroom floor until I heard the key turn in the door. Mike looked surprised to see us that way. He hung up his coat and turned to take a closer look. His mouth widened with surprise when he saw the clump of hair on the floor and my tear-streaked face. I could tell he was starting to say something but I shook my head slightly to indicate we could talk more later. He reached down and scooped the little boy from my arms.

Once they were gone, I slumped against the wall and let the tears flow. My body shook with the sobs of disappointment, fear, and sadness. I sat for a long time, my head pressed to my knees. Sage began to cry, and I finally unfolded my legs and rose to return to the hourly feeding of the newborn. I mixed the formula and wiped another tear from my cheek. Mike returned from putting Alex to bed and took the bottle from my hand. I was relieved as he retrieved the newborn from his swing and began to feed him.

I sat close on the couch still trying to gather my words. "Something isn't right, Mike. It's not normal. It's like he's there and then he's not, you know?"

He nodded his head slowly. "I know."

The next morning Alexander rose with a smile on his face. I placed the book on the table with a roll of tape right next to his breakfast cereal. "We need to fix this book before you go to school today. You'll need to apologize to your teacher too." I braced myself for a fight but he just nodded in response. He asked me to help pull the tape and I did. Joelle and Camille ate quickly and went to the family room to play with the baby. Alexander took slow bites. Breakfast was dragging on forever, and I began to suspect that he was going to miss the bus. I tried to urge him forward but he wouldn't budge. Finally, I felt the nudge of the Holy Spirit. I knew I needed to ask him about his heart. "What are you thinking about, buddy?" He shrugged his shoulders. I tried again. "Are you sad or worried?"

He responded, "Scared. I don't want to get in trouble about the book. I'm going to just tell her that the dog did it."

I sat down next to him. "You know you can't do that. It's a lie."

His voice started to get high and hurried. "Yes it is true. It isn't my fault. It's yours."

I took a deep breath, "You know that isn't true. Would you like me to go with you to tell the teacher?" Once again I was surprised to find that he was actually willing to follow my plan. He nodded and finished his breakfast.

I put the girls on the bus and then buckled the baby seat into the van. Alexander shuffled to the car but allowed me to clip the buckle on the five-point harness. He wouldn't look at me all the way to the school. He wasn't throwing a fit, though, and I counted that as a success. We pulled into the school parking lot, and I realized I could smell the baby. I couldn't believe my bad luck. In all the emotional turmoil, I had forgotten to pack extra diapers in the bag. I knew we had to do this now before the school got too crazy. I wrapped Sage in his blanket and hoped the smell wasn't too horrible.

The teacher welcomed us in just before the bell rang. Alexander stood behind me and peeked around my legs as I spoke. "Thank you for taking the time to talk with us. Alexander would like to tell you something." I stepped aside, but Alexander refused to budge. I could feel my face flush with embarrassment. The baby's diaper was becoming hard to ignore, and I wished desperately that Alexander would just get to the point. The teacher gave me a look that said she didn't appreciate the amount of time it was taking. Finally, I rushed into the conversation. "Alexander wants to apologize for tearing his literacy book. He is very embarrassed. I'm sorry he isn't telling you himself."

She looked down at Alexander and said, "I forgive you. Please be more careful next time." I was relieved. I shook her hand, gave Alex a quick squeeze, and made my way quickly back to the car.

The next few weeks were great with Alexander. We enjoyed his company. He did his homework without complaint and we delighted in his witty humor and compassionate care for his newest brother. I think that's why we answered the call when our caseworker asked if we would be interested in interviewing to adopt two brothers. We were shocked that she asked us, but we knew Sage would be leaving soon and Alexander wanted a brother so badly that we thought there would be no harm in going to the interview.

The following Friday, we entered the DCS office. We both thought there was no way that anyone would pick a crazy family like ours to adopt two more boys. We felt no pressure at all. We even stopped to get coffee on our way. As I opened the double doors, I overestimated the amount of strength it would take and it flew out of my hand. The door hit Mike in the arm, and the coffee went flying across the lobby and hit the wall. Coffee splashed everywhere. I started to laugh and ran to the bathroom to get paper towels. We crawled around the floor wiping up the mess while the other couples watched with tense surprise. We knew we were a spectacle and that made us laugh even harder. We knew it was inappropriate to be laughing, but we just couldn't stop. We apologized to the woman at the front desk, and she was gracious and forgiving.

We had just gained our composure when the caseworker came out to call all the families into the meeting. We were so surprised to find that the grandmothers of the two boys were in the meeting.

They had agreed that the boys should be adopted, and they wanted to make the decision. They told us their story one at a time, and we were moved to tears. Through their stories, we began to love the little boys we had never met. When the grandmothers were done talking we were all released back to the lobby. We were each given an interview time and asked to return. Our time slot was first. We looked at each other. There were no words needed. We knew we wanted them to pick us. We also knew it was a long shot. Mike grabbed my hand as we walked back into the office. "Only God's will," Mike whispered. I squeezed his hand in agreement.

The rest of the day the grandmothers interviewed the other couples while we paced around at home trying to stay busy. We didn't talk about the boys; there was just too much to say and too much at stake. At 5:15 p.m. the phone rang. It was our caseworker. "Hi, Kristin, this is Megan. Is Mike close by? Will you put him on speaker phone?" I waved him over and set the call to speaker. Megan continued, "The grandmothers interviewed all the couples, and even though they originally wanted a home with no other children, they both agreed that you would be the perfect parents for Ezra and Jude. They are here with us right now on this call. What do you say?"

I was overcome. Tears poured from my eyes and my hand was shaking so badly I almost dropped the phone. "Seriously?" I said. I wished I had said something more profound, but that was all I could choke out.

Mike took over. "Yes, we are so excited. Yes. Thank you." The joy poured out of us as we finished the call. We hung up after gathering a few details. Then we just stood and looked at each other for a long time. The kids ran into the room sensing that something had happened. "What is it?" asked Joelle tentatively. "Are you okay?"

I smiled as I answered, "Yes, we are okay. Our family just got picked to adopt two little boys. You're going to be a big sister. You too, Camille. Alexander, you are going to be a big brother!" Alexander looked at us thoughtfully before he replied, "I prayed for one brother and God brought me three."

# CHAPTER 12

# A Sad Happy Sad Homecoming

As is to be expected when fostering, Sage stayed longer than the weekend. He was less than four weeks old when we brought Ezra and Jude home. We met the boys for the first time on a Wednesday. I made the arrangements over the phone with their foster mom, Kathy. I liked her immediately. She was so excited for the children to be finding their forever home. She spoke lovingly about the brothers and their biological family. About 30 minutes into the conversation we discovered we even have the same birthday, although we were born 20 years apart. This was the reason they weren't considering adoption. They felt they had passed that part of their life, but I suspected that they would have been wonderful adoptive parents no matter the circumstance or age.

Mike, Sage, and I arrived in our 12-passenger van and sat in front of the tidy suburban home for a few moments before gathering the courage to go to the door. The other children were at school and Sage was sound asleep in his car seat. We unbuckled him and walked quietly to the door. The family was just as friendly as they had seemed on the phone. They hugged us before we could even cross the threshold. We shrugged out of our coats. It was a mild March day, and the extra layer was beginning to feel suffocating. I handed the coat to my host gratefully and that's when I saw Ezra. His blue eyes were a bright contrast to his wavy brown hair. Jude was in a baby bouncer. He looked at me tentatively and then looked away. The TV was playing a cartoon in the background and the room was filled with brightly colored toys. "Oh, look at this room! I love it. What a wonderful place for them to play!" I exclaimed.

"All the toys belong to the boys. We'll help you load them when you come back tomorrow. We have the cribs for you today though. We took them apart last night and taped the instructions to the crib rails. Is that okay?" Their foster dad, Danny, was directing us toward the garage where he had begun to gather their belongings.

I was in shock. "Where did all this come from?" I gasped.

"Their grandma bought them everything. She spent every penny she had trying to take care of them. She didn't want things to turn out this way. You know?" I nodded in understanding, but I could only imagine how I would feel if I had to place my grandchildren up for adoption one day.

Sage stayed asleep while we talked and planned for the next day's homecoming. I would pick the boys up while the other children were still at school. I saw the tears welling in Kathy's eyes even as she smiled. "I had Ezra when he was first born. We brought him home the same year we brought our daughter home. We weren't going to parent any more children, but she stayed, and we just couldn't let her go. When Ezra went home the first time we were so hopeful for his family. We were happy for them. When he came back into care we were devastated, but glad we could be here to help. Jude is a wonderful addition, but we know we can't raise three babies at our age. We already have Dottie," she gestured to her sweet daughter who now had her arm draped around Ezra's shoulders. I choked up at the sight and looked at Danny. He was in the same state and I discovered I couldn't look anywhere but the floor.

"Please God help me to understand my role in this situation. I feel like I'm taking someone's love away from them. I don't know what to do," I whispered under my breath while Mike talked to Danny.

When I looked up, Kathy was looking me right in my eyes, "We're thankful for you. You know that? We are so glad you're here." I believed her and felt the relief wash over me. I hugged her again and over her shoulder I caught the gaze of my new sons. They were watching.

We loaded the car with toys, cribs, and bright green bedding until there was almost no place to sit. I tightened Sage's car seat into the sliver of bench seat that was left. Dan, Kathy, Mike and I were sweating and laughing by the time we squeezed the van door shut. We hugged one more time like old friends and promised to see one another the next afternoon. Mike and I clicked our seatbelts in silence. I peeked back at Sage and wondered what it might be like to be blissfully unaware. Rain plucked at the windshield. Plink, plink, plink. Slow and steady the rain fell.

I closed my eyes and pictured the faces of my new sons. I said the word in my mind, "sons." I heard Mike click the wipers on, and without opening my eyes, I reached my hand toward the already waiting warmth of his open palm. He squeezed, "It feels weird to be excited about something that is causing so much sadness," he said.

I opened my lids a sliver, "I know."

We didn't talk the rest of the way home, but as we pulled into the driveway, my phone rang. It was my friend Nicole. "Well how did it go?" She asked. "I've been waiting all day. What was it like? What are they like? Are you excited? Worried? Both?" That was one of the things that I loved about this friend. She knew the complexity of human emotions, especially when it came to the constantly changing life of fostering and adoption.

"I don't even know where to begin," I blurted out. I started to tell her about the foster parents, the tears, the blank stares, the stuff, all the stuff.

She said, "Okay, I'm heading over now. We'll get it all set up. It'll be fun." I had to admit, setting up the nursery did sound like fun.

We worked late into the night, and sometime after midnight we stood back and admired the beautifully vibrant nursery. I was so thankful that they were able to sleep against their own sheets and in their own cribs. It would be one bit of home. I would never pick lime green, but it was funny how much I loved the nursery. It represented something so much greater than my own likes, desires, and wishes. It represented the joining of two families into one. They would come with their own personalities and stories. They would also come with two of the greatest grandmothers on the planet. I felt overwhelmed with joy as I clicked the light switch and the room filled with darkness for one last night.

March 11, 2009, I kissed my children as they waited at the bus stop. "When I get home, will my brothers be here?" Alexander looked as if the excitement might escape from his fingertips, toes, and even the ends of his hair.

"Yes, today is the day. You're going to be a big brother!"

He pointed toward Sage who was buckled into the stroller. "I already am a big brother." He rolled his eyes for effect and then hopped up the steps of the school bus. I carried Sage into the house and fed him his bottle in silence. I changed his diaper and dressed him in a light blue velour track suit his birth-mom sent home from the last visit. It was pretty cute, I had to admit. I squeezed his soft cheeks and kissed him on the forehead. "Are you ready for this?" I asked him, expecting no reply from the one-month-old, but he immediately smiled. My heart jumped and I smiled back. Kissing him once more, I grabbed the diaper bag and headed out the door. Our life was about to change. I buckled him into the van once again and made the now-familiar journey to the foster home.

Kathy met me at the door with a warm smile and tear-streaked cheeks. I sat Sage's car seat down in the entry way. "Kathy, is this okay with you? Are you okay? I feel like we are breaking your heart." She wiped a stray tear and reminded me she was sure she was too old to raise all three kids. She wanted the boys to have a home with brothers and sisters and an active family full of life. She loved her role as foster mom. She got to be the person who reunified children with their parents or unified children with their forever families.

She leaned in and told me, "If it doesn't hurt to send the kids home, it's time to stop fostering." I understood what she meant and I believed her. I straightened up, and together we walked into the room where the boys were dressed and ready to go. Ezra continued to look at me thoughtfully with his thumb planted firmly in his mouth. Jude allowed me to pick him up, but his body was stiff as a board. I took Ezra by his free hand. "We're going to go to my house now. I know you're a little nervous. I will do my best to help you feel safe." He nodded once and allowed me to direct him to the car. Kathy helped me load the last of their items and buckle all three boys into the front bench seat of the van. I wanted them close by in case they needed anything. Kathy closed the door and scooped Dottie into her arms. They waved until we were out of sight. Ezra cried silently and Jude screamed in terror.

I pulled over on the side of the road and dug my phone from the diaper bag. I pressed the keys to dial Nicole. "I can't do this." I didn't even wait for her to say hello. "I'm serious, I can't do this. It's not right. How can it be right to take kids from another family they love? I feel selfish and wrong for wanting them to be my sons."

She waited while I sobbed into the phone. When I was done, she asked me where we were. When I told her she responded, "Oh good, I'm right down the street. We should get ice cream. That will make everything better." I couldn't argue with that, so we met up and fed our feelings while the toddlers covered themselves with the sticky mess. They were quiet, which gave me some time to process the pep talk my friend was giving. I did feel better and the kids looked better too. I glanced at my watch and realized the kids and Mike would be home soon. I quickly loaded my three kids into the van and headed for home. Everyone was asleep when we pulled into the driveway. I scooped them from their seats and placed each one into their high chairs just long enough to wipe their hands and faces clean.

Mike and the kids came tumbling through the door just moments later. Jude started screaming again and Ezra whimpered.

I met the kids at the door and explained that the brothers were feeling pretty sad. They all nodded, and I knew that deep within each one of them they felt the loss of their own birth families in that moment. They entered the kitchen cautiously. I raised Ezra from the high-chair and put him on the floor. He immediately put his arms around the dog. Jude clawed his way out of his chair and clung to my arms tightly. With his fists wrapped in my hair, I didn't dare try to put him down. I sat down on the kitchen floor while Mike held Sage and the kids gathered around the dog. The big kids encouraged, "Be gentle Ezra, be careful. She likes it when you pet her like this." They smiled and encouraged Jude too, who eventually patted the dog on the top of her head without letting go of his grip on me.

Our first night home was confusing, scary, sad, and wonderful. I didn't sleep that night. Ezra fell asleep after an hour of rocking, singing, reading, and pure exhaustion. Jude never slept. He continued to cling to me. If I put him down even for a moment, his scream would fill the house and send shivers down my spine. Mike looked at me, helpless to assist. He picked up the slack and put all of the other kids to bed. Kate helped change diapers, brush teeth, and say prayers. I put Jude down once so that I could use the bathroom, but quickly folded him back into my arms even before I finished washing and drying my hands. Jude refused to be rocked or to even sit on my lap. The first night, I paced. I swayed. I climbed up the stairs. I climbed back down. We never slept. The sun came up bright the next morning. Through my exhaustion, I felt a flicker of hope as Jude's lids finally fell heavy.

# CHAPTER 13

# Unexpected Diagnosis

By the time Alexander was seven years old, he had so many diagnoses I couldn't keep them straight. By age four, the pediatrician told us he had ADHD (Attention Deficit Hyperactivity Disorder). By age five, we were told he had RAD (Reactive Attachment Disorder) and ODD (Oppositional Defiant Disorder.) By six years old, we tacked on an Anxiety Disorder, PTSD (Post Traumatic Stress Disorder), and there was talk of BPD (Borderline Personality Disorder). Each appointment ended with more labels. He was a hoarder; he was impulsive; he had a low IQ. We heard the labels and felt the burden each one carried. Hyperactive, inattentive, anxious, insomnia. The hope seeped out of me as the list of verdicts grew longer and longer. No one had an answer.

The pediatrician insisted that cocaine and marijuana exposure in utero did not have any lasting effects. She suggested that we just didn't know how to parent a boy. It hurt, but we accepted our place as less knowledgeable. She wanted to start him on medicine as he entered first grade. We blindly followed her advice, trying three medications, with each magnifying the problem. We repeatedly asked if maybe the drug and alcohol exposure could have caused this. She adamantly denied that substance abuse had any lasting effects on children. She assured us that even babies born addicted to cocaine quickly grew out of the addiction and went on to lead healthy, productive lives. She again asked if we were taking parenting classes. She looked at his sweet face and told me he looked fine to her. When she told me I just didn't understand his culture and suggested he needed a black male in his life to act as a father figure, I left the office shaking. I never went back.

Alexander's behavioral upsets steadily increased in frequency and severity. During a home visit with Alexander's Department of Child Services caseworker, I brought up my concerns. I was desperate to find services that would help with his increasingly aggressive behavior. She looked me up and down slowly as I spoke. When I finished describing his behavior and my concerns for his safety, she responded, "If you can't handle him, we'll find a family that can."

I felt a thick lump form in my throat. "No, I can handle him. I'm sure he just needs a little more supervision. I'm fine. Thank you for your time." I closed the door behind her and with it closed my heart to the hope of finding help.

The elementary school found that they could not help Alexander succeed. He could not retain information. He could not comprehend what he was reading and did not understand simple math concepts even by second grade. They called each day with concerns about his inability to sit in a chair, make friends, and pass any standardized tests. We found support at his school, but still no answers. He eventually began to spend most of his day in a self-contained classroom. He hated being separate from his peers and grew increasingly aggressive toward his teachers and other staff.

When Alexander was seven years old, Jude had just turned two. Jude didn't sleep for the first year he lived with us. One entire year. No sleep. His body was rigid and he rarely made eye contact. He became frustrated easily, and when he was frustrated he would stand straight and drop to the floor smacking his head so hard I thought it might split open. I was certain that he was doing damage to his tiny brain with all the head banging, breath holding, and lack of sleep. Jude was fussy and red-faced for most of that first year. His body was covered in eczema and he scratched until his skin bled.

Mike and I found that we could prevent the head banging by buckling Jude into an infant-size life jacket. He seemed to like the pressure of the vest, and if he decided to fall to the floor, the jacket cushioned his fall. We sewed the ends of his shirts together to prevent the skin picking. First Steps came to our house every day with a different therapy for Jude. We learned a lot about Occupational Therapy, Physical Therapy, Speech Therapy, and Developmental Therapy. Our therapists became our lifeline to hope. Jude made progress but we still couldn't understand the root of the behaviors. We knew he had been through trauma, but similar to Alexander, there was so much more there. So many layers to peel back, we wondered if we would ever see the true character of our little son.

One day while visiting with the biological family of Jude, we learned that his birth mom had been drinking throughout her pregnancy and even had to be forced to stop breastfeeding while intoxicated. Something about that information clicked for me. Jude didn't match the picture I had in my mind of a child exposed to alcohol. I went to my computer late that night and began to search drug and alcohol exposure. What I found shocked me. It was contradictory to what I had been told by the pediatrician, caseworkers, and even therapists in our life. I read late into the night. Jude was displaying the classic symptoms of alcohol exposure. I called a friend who worked at our children's hospital the next day. She knew of a doctor at the hospital who had opened a fetal alcohol clinic. She connected me with the information we needed and I got the referral that week from our new pediatrician.

The day of our appointment, I sent our other children off to school and to the babysitter's house. Everyone except Alexander and Jude. Alexander had thrown a mega tantrum that morning and refused to get on the bus. He was anxious and agitated. To this day, I'm not sure why I gave in to his clinginess. Looking back, I believe the hand of the Lord was on us the moment I decided to take him with me. I held him as he calmed down. Watching the clock, I worried that we wouldn't make it to the appointment on time.

Alexander's heartrate began to slow and his breathing returned to normal. I looked at him and said, "Come on, let's get in the car. I need your help with Jude today. He has to go to the doctor and you know how afraid he gets at the doctor's office." Alexander nodded and buckled himself into the seat next to Jude. We rode in peace all the way to the hospital and made it just in time for our appointment. As anyone with children knows, appointments are never on time. We waited for an hour in the waiting room and by the time we were called back, I had run completely out of Cheerios and Goldfish crackers. The boys were antsy and tired.

The nurse tried to get Jude's height and weight but when I tried to remove him from my arms, he screamed and grabbed a fistful of hair. Alexander tried to help his little brother, but he couldn't get through. He spoke softly to him, "Jude, it's okay, little brother. They just need to see how big you are. You're fine. We're right here with you." I was so proud of Alexander, but Jude would not be placed on the scale. I felt myself beginning to sweat. I could feel the heat of embarrassment rising in my cheeks. The nurse stopped and placed her hand on my arm, "It's okay, we understand. This happens all the time here." Those simple words unleashed the tears I was holding back. I tried to compose myself while she grabbed a tissue for me. "That happens all the time here too." She assured me.

Everyone in the office was helpful, kind, and patient. I felt heard and cared for. It was incredibly freeing to not feel like this was somehow my fault. The doctor looked over every inch of Jude's body and the appointment took a full hour. He never rushed, but carefully analyzed Jude's ears, nose, eyes, palms, and toes. He asked questions about every aspect of his behavior and habits. He explained how the diagnosis works. "There is no test for Fetal Alcohol Exposure. There is a spectrum of disorders that can be caused by exposure to alcohol. It is helpful if we have a first-hand witness to Mom's drinking. Even when we don't, we know that alcohol is the most readily accessible, inexpensive, legal drug available. If Mom had substance abuse issues, it is safe to assume she used alcohol as well. We will compile all of the data we collect today to determine where Jude falls on the spectrum." I had been told so often that drinking left no long-term damage that this information was a complete shift in thinking. I had known all along that my children were experiencing the effects of exposure, but this was the first time I felt validated.

The validation was not as satisfying as I hoped it would be. Jude was tired and so was Alexander. The appointment had taken the entire morning and we were all getting a little hungry. Hearing the doctor's determination that Jude had in fact been exposed to alcohol and was suffering the results of his birth mother's drinking, sent a painful shock through my system. I pictured him in utero, unable to escape the poison all around him. I saw the pictures of what his brain looked like and I felt sick at the thought. I loved his birth mom. Jude has the bluest eyes and the longest eyelashes I've ever seen. When we are in public, people stop to comment on the stunning beauty of his eyes. It is a feature he gets directly from his first mother. He has her eyes. I love that about him, but now I felt a mix of anger and bitter frustration at her choices.

Throughout the appointment, I had not realized that I was wrestling Alexander at every turn. It had become a part of my every-day life to have one hand and one eye always on Alex. I handed him at least 15 objects out of the diaper bag, each holding his attention for mere minutes. I fed him snacks and drinks until there wasn't a crumb left and I shushed him constantly with a finger to my lips. He sat on my lap, on the floor, on the back of the chair. Then he stood on his head, spun in circles, and pulled all the paper off the examination table. He played with Jude, keeping him occupied and then lost interest and growled at me, demanding to leave. It was frustrating, but I was so in tune to Jude's appointment it didn't even dawn on me that his behavior was inappropriate for a doctor's office.

As I dressed Jude and prepared to leave, the doctor looked at me in a way that caught my full attention. "Have you already had him diagnosed?"

I wrinkled my brow as I looked in the direction he was pointing. "Alexander?" The doctor nodded. "No, I, well, should I?"

The doctor nodded politely. "You can make an appointment on your way out for me to see him as well." I felt like the wind had been knocked out of me. I was at once overwhelmed by the sad realization that my precious sons were both about to be diagnosed with something that had no cure and that they had no possibility of growing out of. I was also filled with a new and very clear sense of hope. It wasn't the solution I was looking for, but it was an actual answer. For the first time since bringing both of them home, I had the possibility of actually understanding where they were coming from.

**CHAPTER 14**

# Hoarding, Stealing, and Loneliness

By the time Alexander was in preschool we noticed his tendency toward being a pack rat. He hid anything and everything under his pillow or beneath his mattress. Before I could put anything into the washer, I had to empty each and every pocket. This could sometimes take an unbelievable amount of time. Anyone who has ever cleaned out a dryer after a run-in with a green crayon, knows that the initial extra effort is worth avoiding the inevitable melted mess.

We suspected he was taking things from other students as we helped him unpack his backpack each afternoon. There were always one or two items that we knew didn't belong to him. One day it might be a handful of paper clips, the next day a Superman lunchbox, a different pair of socks, a freshly sharpened #2 pencil. We insisted that he return the items each day, but making things right became overwhelming. He took an apple from his teacher's desk. He took a snack from a kid on the bus. If the items made it past us at the front door, we would eventually find them in his room. He wasn't sneaky about the taking. One night at dinner he produced a handful of Lego figures and began setting up a battlefield across his plate using his fork as a gun. "Alexander, where did you get those?" I inquired.

"They're mine!" He shouted. "Why do you always ask me that?"

I took a deep breath as I tried to gain control over my frustration. "You don't own any Legos, Alexander." He pouted and threw the Legos and the plate off the table. We returned the items to his teacher the next day. The anxiety over the stealing grew, and I dreaded facing each new parent, teacher, or bus driver with the truth.

Alexander had lost more than a few friends by the beginning of elementary school. He was never invited to a birthday party. I mean, never. When he was in third grade, we sat on our back deck grilling hamburgers and hot dogs. The kids were playing in our backyard. The air had just turned chilly and we were soaking up every last bit of sun before the winter hit. Our neighbors were doing the same. We could see into the yards of our other neighbors. They were grilling out, pulling weeds, dividing bulbs, mowing the lawn one last time. It seemed like everyone was out

Alexander's friend lived three houses away, and his backyard was more full than normal. Children were jumping on the trampoline and chasing one another through the backyard. I recognized the kids and looked a little closer. My smile quickly faded. They were Alexander's classmates. His friend's mom carried out a large cake filled with candles. The children rushed toward her and began singing. I realized everyone was invited but my son. I paused and rationalized that he may have forgotten the invitation in his book bag. I went inside and dug everything out, knowing there was no way I missed it during our daily checks. Nothing. I knew why he hadn't been invited. I knew without anyone telling me. The rejection hurt more than I could handle. I looked at Mike and pointed over to the party, "Let's go inside before he notices." Mike nodded and we gathered our dinner and our children and went inside to hide.

I debated walking over and giving the neighbor a piece of my mind. I settled the kids at the table. They chewed and smiled and made conversation. Alexander happily spread more than his share of catsup on his burger and I fumed. Jude looked over at me and tilted his head to the side, "Are you sad, Mommy?"

I forced a smile, "No way, baby, I'm good. This is a yummy dinner. Did you all tell Daddy thank you?" They all turned to their father and thanked him. I fumed even more. *We are nice people,* I thought to myself. Why are we always getting left out of things? I scooted my chair back and excused myself, "I'll be right back." I walked to the door. I skipped the shoes and exited quickly. I made my way down the sidewalk — one house, two houses, three. I turned back. I quickly stepped back onto my front porch. Words swirling in my mind, I paced for a minute and headed back down the front steps. One house, two houses, three, pause. I looked at the front door of my neighbor. I heard the happy squeals of the party kids. I clenched and unclenched my fists. I turned back. I paced on my front porch for another minute and exited once again down the driveway — only this time I turned left away from the happy birthday party, away from the exclusiveness, away from the hurt.

I picked up the pace and soon felt my feet hitting the pavement rhythmically. I balled up my fists and heard my heart pounding in my chest. It felt as if it might explode. I ran full speed. All I wanted to do was escape the reality. I ran away from the anger. I shook off the isolation. I sprinted toward the darkness that lay beyond my neighborhood. The sun was setting and I knew there weren't sidewalks along the newly empty cornfields. I kept going. The darkness swallowed me, and it felt welcome. Tears filled my eyes and overflowed my lids, streaming down my cheeks. I didn't stop to wipe them. It felt good to feel the cool air against my tear-stained cheeks. Eventually, I stopped. For no particular reason, I realized I was done running. I put my hands on my knees and caught my breath. I turned around and began the long walk home. The coldness in my feet began to register in my consciousness, and I identified more than a few scrapes. My walk turned to a limp as my neighborhood came into view. That's what my life felt like — a limp.

I wanted my son to be invited to the party, but I knew in my heart why he wasn't invited. He tried to play with the neighbor many times, but always came home with something that didn't belong to him. Just a few weeks earlier he had shoved a pair of brand new tennis shoes under his bed. When the other little boy's mom showed up at our door the next morning, I was confused. As soon as she asked for her son's tennis shoes I realized her discomfort. She didn't want to tell me that she suspected my son of stealing, "I think Preston left his shoes here, would you mind looking for them?" She averted her eyes and I knew that she knew they had been stolen like so many things before. I immediately went to Alexander's room and reached under the bed. He never even tried to find better hiding places. It was always the same. I didn't have the energy to say anything. I just handed her the shoes and waved goodbye. I knew why he hadn't been invited to the party, but it still hurt.

Alexander seemed to have no understanding of how others perceived his need to take things. We tried to explain each time we watched him have to return an item, but he would stand firm in his conviction that the items were actually his. He was only angry with us and never felt any obligation to consider the feelings of others. We found ourselves disturbed by his lack of empathy. He would walk out of his brothers' room with pockets bulging and look surprised when asked to return the items he'd taken. Missing objects became an everyday part of our existence. As Alexander matured, so did his system for getting things he wanted. He still took items from others, but by junior high he had graduated to begging.

One day he came home with a very expensive smart phone. We were shocked and demanded to know where it came from. This led to a standoff that lasted hours. We changed our tactic, remembering that he needed us to stay calm when he didn't have the ability to grasp reality. We tried approaching him differently, "Hey, you aren't in trouble right now. We just need to know where the phone came from."

He glared at us, "From someone who actually cares about me!" My heart quickened as I thought of some predator luring him in with the promise of a phone.

I forced myself not to over-react. "I just need to know who gave it to you. People don't give gifts like that. It's too expensive." I paused and worked up the courage to ask, "Was it an adult? Where did you meet the person?" He paced back and forth in front of us.

My husband jumped in as he noticed I was beginning to panic. "Where did you get it, buddy? Mom and I are just a little worried."

He stopped the pacing abruptly and shouted, "Aiden gave it to me! His family cares about him. His family doesn't let him feel left out all the time. Everyone has a phone, but you guys hate me. You never give me anything I want!" I sucked in another breath. Aiden was another student in his special education class.

I picked up my own phone and sent a quick text to Aiden's mom. She got right back to me and promised to ask her son. "I'm checking with Aiden's mom right now," I said.

Alexander began to cry, "He didn't want me to be left out. Other kids were making fun of me." The return text confirmed Alexander's story. We apologized and promised to return the phone that night. No matter what we provided Alexander, he always felt that he had been denied.

The fear of not having enough was never more present than when food was involved. By early elementary we discovered that if the pantry and refrigerator were left unlocked, Alexander would eat everything. One night he woke after we were all asleep and ate half of a jar of peanut butter and then threw up. We wouldn't have known about it except we were startled awake by the sound of him vomiting. When we ran to help him, we found the half-eaten jar in his room. We could not seem to find a way to help him connect his full belly with his worried mind. When Alexander was a baby there truly hadn't been enough food. His brain became wired in those first months to expect to have to fight for every morsel. Try as we might, we could not unwire the connections he had to food and the fear of not having enough.

We began to notice Alexander was acting more fearful instead of less as time went on. We showed him the pantry. We included him in packing lunches each day and preparing the meals to eat at home. He loved being the helper, but still couldn't calm his own anxieties over food. We were completely at a loss by the time we realized he had been making his rounds during the school day telling different teachers that he was hungry. They had no reason not to trust him and it didn't occur to them that he may be struggling with an insecurity in his heart not an emptiness in his belly. For weeks, he was getting the nurse to give him a granola bar and the special education teacher to give him a handful of crackers. He was talking the lunch lady into a second helping of food even though he had documentation on his lunch account that stated that he was only supposed to eat the lunch that was provided from home. They too trusted his perspective and saw the growing boy in front of them who was just hungry for one more small snack. The adults in his life didn't see the harm in what they were doing. They didn't understand that every time they fed his body they created a greater insecurity in his mind. His brain was fixed on the thought that moms and dads don't feed their kids. He couldn't shake the feeling that Mike and I did not have his best interest in mind. He was certain that he was in a fight for survival.

We began to learn about brain development through an organization in our town which offered post adoption services. We began to understand how our son's brain had been formed in a way that solidified mistrust at the core. We then began to see our son's hoarding, stealing, and lying as something other than a behavior. It was a reaction to a hurt that was stuck in a part of his consciousness that he could not access or understand. We talked with a therapist who encouraged us to physically show Alex the food he would eat for the day. We began packing him a backpack filled with food to carry with him at school or on car trips. He had healthy options that he could choose throughout the day. We were empowered to educate our son's teachers on our perspective, and we soon found that with their support, Alexander began to view food in a different way. With their reassurance that moms and dads do provide for their children, Alexander was often able to steer his emotions away from the panic and learn trust for us. The stealing and hoarding will always be a tendency that Alexander has, remnants of the fear he was born into, but they do not have to define him.

# CHAPTER 15

# Rage Monster

One summer, as the months dragged on, I found myself struggling to fill the days. We hiked in the woods every single morning. Even in the rain, we ventured outside to meander the wooded trails. Sage loved to be the leader. He was only four, but he quickly took the lead whenever possible. I knew I would have to force him to allow someone else to lead the way for once. Around 8:30 we piled out of the 12-passenger van and into the already muggy July morning. Sage was barefoot again. I started to open my mouth to tell him to head back for his shoes, then I thought the better of it. I slipped mine off too and put them under the driver's seat. Jude reached up for my hand as I closed and locked the double doors. Ezra had already darted ahead of everyone. He ducked beneath the low branches of a willow tree and crouched down with his face near to the ground. Alexander caught up with him first and got onto his belly in the tall grass. Camille, Joelle, and Sage scurried to catch up. I trotted along behind all of them still holding the hand of Jude.

"Momma!" Ezra called without moving a muscle. "Momma, come here." I came into view and lowered my head to see what was going on. The kids sat still next to a nest of the tiniest baby rabbits. They were pink and fuzzy, their eyes weren't even open yet.

"Oh, they are so little," I gasped. "I've never seen them so tiny." We stayed for a while just watching them. All the children were mesmerized. Alexander barely moved a muscle. He stayed flat on his belly and just watched. In a typical day I have to tell Alexander not to touch things approximately one million times. Not this day.

I was too busy watching my children to notice the lifeless body of the rabbit lying just past the branches of the tree. Joelle noticed it first. She gasped and immediately began to cry. "Oh no! Oh no, Mommy! It's dead, it's dead, it's dead. Momma, the babies have no momma. I know that was their mom." She could not catch her breath. and I couldn't move the children fast enough. I shushed her and put my arms around her, but it was too late. Camille was turned away from us with arms folded, staring blankly back at our car. Ezra had his thumb in his mouth, with large tears spilling over his cheeks. Jude furrowed his brow and spoke only in a growling voice. Sage climbed into my arms and put his arms around Joelle's neck. I assured them that these things happen and it's just a part of life, I heard my own voice catch even as I tried to explain the sadness to my children.

"It's okay, Mommy, I've got them. I won't let them go. I know what it's like to lose a mom and it stinks. It's a good thing we found them. We are the kind of family who helps when people need a mom, right, Momma?" My eyes snapped up to see Alexander cradling three baby rabbits in the fabric of his shirt.

"Oh, no!" I said, "We don't know anything about caring for bunnies." It was too late though. I knew we couldn't leave them here to die. "Okay, don't worry, guys, we'll figure out what to do." Alexander refused to put them down, so we walked carefully back to the car. We buckled in and traveled home to do a little research. We brought the bunnies inside. Joelle and Alexander prepared them a small shoebox filled with grass clippings. Camille covered it with a kitchen towel and placed them on a top shelf, far out of the reach of the dogs and of little brothers. We knew they couldn't stay forever; we didn't have the means to care for them. I quickly logged into the Internet to search for answers. I found out that there are only a handful of wildlife rescues in the area. I called each of them.

The first two women apologized immediately, "We're just too full right now. I don't have anyone to care for them." I understood and hung up the phone. Running my finger down the list of names, I came to one more in our county. The line went directly to a voicemail. I explained the situation again and left my number. I was discouraged, and I was getting worried that Alexander was going to do more harm than good. He had climbed up on the shelf to check on the babies no less than ten times while I made the call. He lifted the blanket and shook as his hand hovered over the tiny creatures. I knew he desperately wanted to touch them. I shook my head at him again. He sighed and pulled his hand away from the box.

I turned as the phone rang. I answered on the second ring, still shaking my head at Alex. As I spoke to the woman, I watched my son climb one last time up the shelf. I shook my head again vigorously. He made eye contact with me and shook his head back, then reached into the box and produced one of the minuscule rabbits. I made the meanest face I could while trying to keep my voice cheerful. The woman on the other end had a raspy tone and an unkind demeanor. She harshly repeated the directions to me one more time as Alexander walked out the back door still carrying the rabbit.

I hung up the phone and raced after my son. "Please put that bunny back. You are going to hurt it," I said sternly.

"No, I won't," he responded as he shrugged his shoulders. His hand was squeezing tighter around the rabbit. I took a step back and made the request again. "I know you don't want to hurt that animal. You are a loving person. I need you to put it back where it's safe." The argument went back and forth for another 15 minutes. Finally, he handed over the rabbit and called me a horrible name. I snapped and shouted back. I hated myself for it, and I was immediately sorry. He stuck his middle finger up at me and dodged out of the yard screaming.

I placed the rabbit back in the box and turned toward the house. I was so tired of chasing him. I hated the feeling of always being on edge, uncertain when he would blow up. So often the tantrums were triggered by some unknown factor. He was loving one moment and hateful the next. I shut the door behind me as a brick hit the side of the house. My heart pounded and fear surged through me. I screamed for the kids, "Safety plan, upstairs now! Do not challenge me on this." Thankfully, they didn't. I handed Camille the box and asked her to carry it upstairs as well. They locked themselves behind the hallway door and then my bedroom door as well. Knowing they were safe was always the first step. I felt better.

I looked out the window to see where he was. He was pacing on the back porch, cursing. I opened the door and was immediately assaulted with the most unkind words. He threatened to kill me and all his brothers and sisters. He threatened to jump off the roof and kill himself. "When I get older, I'll get a gun and there's nothing you can do about it. I'll kill all of you."

The coldness filled me with despair, then fear, and finally anger. I knew better than to allow myself to react, but I did. I was horrified with myself as I responded out of my own hurt and rage. "I don't care about you either," I said in a low voice. "I don't care. I'm sick of your words. I'm sick of the way you hurt people. Why don't you run away for real? Stop pretending and just do it already." I felt as if my body detached from my soul. I hated that I had just said that, but my fists were clenched and my vision narrowed. I didn't even register his words. I just saw anger and felt anger. The emotion filled the space and I demanded that he go inside. He refused of course, but I demanded anyway.

I knew that I needed to stop talking, but I couldn't stop. I demanded and threatened. I swore I would take his toys away or ground him from his bike. He didn't care. He shook his head back at me and tried different combinations of swear words to see what would get the most reaction. Some of the words were almost comical, but I didn't laugh. I warned again, and he lunged at me. He put his hands around my throat and began to squeeze. I was shocked back into reality. I picked him up, loosened his grip on my neck, and wrapped my arms around his, holding his elbows to his side. I carried him through the door and into the living room. I put my knee behind his leg and proceeded to put him into the therapeutic hold that his therapist taught me. I lowered his body to the floor and sat behind him with arms wrapped around his and legs crossed across his. He fought and bit and wiggled his hands free a few times. I kept taking deep breaths and tried to stay focused on calm. I started to talk out loud through my own thoughts. "I don't know what happened there. I don't understand. We had such a nice day today. Things were going fine. I was mad at you for taking the bunny out, but I'm not mad anymore. I don't understand why you flipped on me. I don't understand."

He responded to the conversation with spit and drool and swear words. I wasn't doing anything to help. I knew I was at fault for snapping in the first place, but it was too late to go back. I apologized, never taking my hands off him.

Alexander kept going for two more hours. I was exhausted, but I wasn't going to give up. I kept talking calmly and I apologized many more times for what I had said. I cried until my eyes were puffy. He cried too, but didn't lessen the fierceness of his fight. At one point his arms went limp and he looked me in the eye and said calmly, "I'm done." I let go, and he immediately grabbed a handful of my hair and pulled. I screamed and put my arms back around him, pinning him next to my body. He began the entire episode over from the beginning again.

I was starting to get tired when Joelle came down the stairs to check on me. She was upset and angry. "I hate living like this!" she screamed.

"I know, I know, honey. I'm sorry this is happening again. How are your brothers?" I could feel the absurdity of having this conversation as if I didn't have my entire body wrapped around another person whose singular goal was to hurt someone.

She answered, "They're hungry and tired of this too." I knew they were and walked Joelle through the steps of buying a pizza. She took my phone and called the number. She was so mature about the whole thing that I began to cry again. My children had witnessed so many of these meltdowns that they had come to see this as a normal part of life. This was unacceptable, and I knew it.

Our 12-pound dachshund came bounding around the corner just as Joelle returned upstairs to retrieve money for the pizza. The tiny dog barreled through the dining room and dove on top of Alexander. She burrowed her face beneath Alexander's arm, and I immediately felt his heart begin to slow. His breathing became less ragged and he started to pet her with the tips of his fingers. I didn't dare let his arms go, but I said, "You scared her, she wants you to feel safe and she needs to feel safe too."

I began to pray out loud as Alexander's body relaxed. "Lord, Alex needs You. He needs to know he is safe. You have created him for a purpose. You have made him in Your image. He is meant to be so much more than this rage. Lord, Alex doesn't trust me, and that's okay. I really hurt him tonight with what I said. I hope that one day he will be able to forgive me. I don't understand this rage. I don't understand this anger right now. Father, I need Your guidance. I need You to show me the way with Alex. Please show us both the way. Amen."

Alexander was now making eye contact with me. His body felt calm, and I cautiously removed my arms from his. "I forgive you, Mom. Do you forgive me?"

I did forgive him, but I felt uneasy as the evening wore on. We paid for the pizza and ate together in time to meet the lady from the rescue with the rabbits. I squeezed everyone's hand while we prayed together, and then we set out once again in the van for another adventure. By then Mike was home from work. We told him all about the day we'd had. Alex was contrite and didn't challenge anyone as we traveled onto the country roads to find help for our little furry friends.

As we drove, Mike wrinkled his forehead and stared out at the vastness of the fields in front of us. He looked as if he was searching for something. He was quiet as we released the rabbits and wished the rescuer good luck. He was quiet as we journeyed toward home. "Hey, Alexander, I was thinking about something. Did those bunnies make you think about what happened to you when you lost your birth-mom?" Alexander didn't respond at first but the look on his face showed a flicker of recognition. We drove on as I saw one tear trickle down his face.

CHAPTER 16

# Good Life

The song "Good Life" by One Republic was popular the summer Alexander was placed in residential treatment. I loved that song. It played constantly, and I never could get enough of it. The eight of us would sing along at the top of our lungs, rocking out in our 12-passenger van. The song filled me with a mix of melancholy, hope, and joy combined.

After ten days in the adolescent psychiatric ward, Alexander was no closer to returning home than he had been when we admitted him. He was combative and angry and refused to take responsibility for himself. We were still trying medication at the time and the psychiatrist had concocted a cocktail of meds that would knock a grown man off his feet. Still, nothing seemed to take the edge off for Alex. I was allowed to visit him every other day. Mike and I took turns visiting. He had a strict wardrobe of pants with elastic waistbands lacking buttons or ties. Slip-on shoes with no laces and pullover t-shirts. We would collect his clothes and replace them with freshly laundered outfits.

Each time we visited we had to fill out a form listing our goals. There was a section for parents, one for the child, and one for the family. I would grab my form and sit down next to Alexander. He refused to look at me. "Hey, little man, it's so good to see you today. Did you use the comb I packed you? I made sure you have the lotion you like, and I packed your slippers today."

He perked up at the mention of slippers. "Where are they?" he asked without taking his eyes off a pair of younger teens playing a board game. I reached into the bag and produced the pair that Mike and I found for him the previous Christmas. They were exactly like Mike's, and Alexander loved that he had some shoes just like his daddy. He took them from me without gratitude and slipped them onto his stocking feet. I pointed to the form and said, "Are you ready to do this?" He shook his head slightly, "I don't care. Do it if you want to."

I waited a bit before responding. I changed the subject, "Do you want to play cards?" I slowly moved his face toward me, and he looked me in the eye.

"Nope," was his simple reply. I shook off the negativity.

The entire 30-minute visit seemed to drag on, each silent minute feeling like an hour. "Look, I know you're mad at me. I hate that you're here, but I needed to keep you safe. Things aren't safe at home like this. Can we please talk about this?" The silence drug on until the staff supervisor called the parents to be dismissed. I willed my son to connect with me, but I didn't say anything more. Parents gathered at the double steel doors and, sensing my cue, I rose slowly. I placed my hand on my son's arm and squeezed slightly then turned to walk away.

I met with the psychologist the following day privately. She shook her head as she looked over Alexander's files. "He just isn't willing to work here. I'm afraid if he returns home, he will hurt himself or someone else," she said gently. A flood of relief washed over me it was good to have someone believe what we had been saying for a long time. The relief was quickly followed by regret and guilt. I instantly wanted her to say that we were mistaken. I wished she would hand me the solution I so desperately desired. I wanted all of this not to be true. I longed to run and grab my son and pull him into my arms like I did when he was small, whispering in his ear how much I loved him. I couldn't; we were separated by thick walls, locked doors, and years of hurt. "It may be time to think about residential treatment," she continued with a gentle ease.

"I know." I choked out the only words I could. Blessedly, she took the lead and talked me through each possibility. I took every brochure and shook her hand. I shuffled from the building in a daze.

That night Mike and I tucked the other children into bed and placed the brochures on the kitchen table. We sat there for a long time without talking. Finally, we gripped hands and prayed for our son. When the night was over we had made the decision.

The hospital released Alexander the following day, but there would not be a space for our son at the treatment center for three more days. The psychologist expressed surprise when we shared that we wanted to take him home and transport him to the center on our own. We wanted him to know that this decision was made out of concern and love. We wanted to look in our son's face and tell him that we had a plan and that we would never abandon him no matter what. She nodded as we talked and then helped us complete the paperwork for his release.

The three of us rode in silence all the way home. When we entered the house, we were greeted by five cautious children. They stood back and watched him as he walked to the living room and flopped onto the couch. The next three days were edgy. We explained our decision, which was met with frustration, sadness, and anger. I slept next to his bed on the floor just like I had when he was a baby. I didn't want to miss a moment with my baby. I wrestled each night as the moon rose high outside of his window. I reached my hand onto the edge of his twin bed and ran my fingers through his hair. In the moonlight, I could only see the baby I loved.

We watched fireworks on his last day home. He curled up in my lap and we both looked up toward the night sky. *Oh God*, I pleaded, *please change this circumstance. Please take this from us.* My arms wrapped around his tiny frame. I breathed in his scent, a mix of shampoo and dirt. Just a typical boy, my boy, my son.

Mike had to be out of town the day the center would admit Alexander. He would be two hours in the opposite direction so we agreed to meet in the middle. I was relieved to have my parents in town to watch the other children while we traveled. I slept fitfully that last night with my son. I begged the Lord to give me a different answer. I cried out through the night and laid flat on my face in surrender. I doubted all the years that had led up to this. Maybe this was all my fault. If I had done something differently, possibly I could have prevented this. I knew to my core that I must be the worst mother ever. I didn't know of anyone who had made a choice this terrible. I found myself certain that I was completely and utterly alone in all of this.

I woke that morning to screaming. I opened my puffy eyes and took inventory of the situation. Alexander was not lying beside me. I felt terror rush through me, and taking the stairs two at a time I flew to the kitchen. Alexander was perched on the counter with a glass jar over his head. On the floor, the contents of the breakfast I had planned were scattered.

"Please get down," I said firmly.

"NO!" he yelled with everything in him. He flew from the counter to the island in one huge leap. I turned to see Joelle standing protectively in front of Ezra with her arms open wide. "Joelle, please take Ezra upstairs and get Grandma and Grandpa," I urged. She refused with a firm shake of her head, never taking her eyes off of Alexander. "Joelle, safety plan. Please follow the safety plan. I'm fine. Everything will be fine." Reluctantly, she scooped Ezra into her tiny arms and edged out of the kitchen, meeting my mom on the stairs.

"We're okay, Mom. Will you please get the other kids?" I asked.

"Yes, I've got them. Are you okay?" I could see her concern.

Just then Alexander slipped by me and into the garage. I followed while taking deep breaths. The door slammed in my face, and it startled me. I turned the knob in a rush and flung the door open to the sight of a pitchfork right in my face. "Don't come near me," he snarled. I backed up a step and began to pray again for my son. This time not pleading for a different direction but for safety. I prayed for his and mine. My heart was pounding, and my chest felt that it would burst with the fear.

Sweat dripped down my brow and I spoke in an unnaturally calm voice, "Alexander, I need you to put the pitch fork down. It's really dangerous." His pupils were so large his eyes looked black. I didn't break eye contact. "I don't want you to hurt someone. I'm worried about you. You seem really upset."

He responded in a whisper that scared me more than the yelling, "I'm not *trying* to hurt you. I am *going* to hurt you." I felt the pounding in my chest stop. For a moment I couldn't force my lungs to take another breath. When I finally did, I sucked in the air that seemed to have exited the garage. It wasn't enough. I felt dizzy.

I prayed again, but this time I had no words, "Help. Help me. Help him. Help." I said the last word out loud, "Help, Jesus, please help." Alexander looked startled but kept his eye on me, and his fists firmly grasping the tool.

I regained my calm and spoke to him as if this were any typical day. "Alexander, I know that today is a scary day for you. It is for me too. I'm worried, and you are worried. I don't want you to go to this place, but the behavior you are having is really dangerous. Daddy and I can't keep you safe when you are doing this. We can't keep your brothers and sisters safe either. I'm sad this is happening. It's okay for you to be sad too. This place will help all of us to keep you safe. You won't stay forever, it's just for a while. I'm still your mom, and you will always be my son. I know you're worried. There is nothing you can do to stop making me be your mom. Not even what you are doing now. I love you so much, I will do anything to help you, even the things that hurt."

Alexander put the pitchfork down slowly. "I don't want to go," he said.

"I know, but this will only be for a short time. If you work hard and learn a lot, you will be able to come home more quickly. Okay?

I'm going to get your breakfast and bring it in the car with us. Why don't you get in your seat and calm down. I packed everything for you last night. All your special things are there." To my surprise he buckled himself into the front seat without a fight.

I grabbed two granola bars and hugged my mom quickly. I pulled out of the driveway without saying goodbye to the other children. My heart pulled two ways, but I knew I needed to get us on the road while Alexander was feeling compliant. Our town slipped away and we wound around the country roads heading north. In one small town we spotted a bakery with a drive through. I pulled over and ordered two glazed donuts, a coffee, and an orange juice. My head still spinning from the drama, I turned to hand him his treat and was met with the sweetest smile. "Thanks, Mom," he said without prompting. I couldn't look at him and quickly turned my eyes back to the road.

We flew along the open roads and marveled at the beauty of the barns, cornfields, and wind turbines. For endless miles the turbines stretched and spun in the mild July breeze. My eyes felt heavy, and I glanced over to see my son sleeping. "Good Life" came on the radio just at that moment. "This has got to be a good life. . . ." The song felt right, my sweet son sleeping beside me. My hand reached toward him and hesitated. I didn't want to wake him, but I felt a deep sense that I needed to fold my arms around him like I did when he was a baby. I wanted to protect him; to seal that peaceful moment into my mind forever. The tears fell in streams. This was my last day with my baby, and I knew it. This was the end of what was before. I hoped there would be good in the future, but that lay uncertain. What I did know was that we had to get help; we had to leave some of the bad behind. It was time. The song played on, and I traced his fingers with my own. The song played on, and I let go of the past. I faced our future as the corn and soybeans again rolled by my window.

# CHAPTER 17

# Unexpected Peace

Alexander spent four months at his first residential treatment facility. He worked with a wonderful woman who taught our entire family coping skills and a new way to communicate. Each Saturday we made the three-hour trip to see him and each Saturday night we made the three-hour trip home.

Our home life was peaceful during that time, but our hearts were torn. We each wrote him letters and drew him pictures every day. We talked to him on the phone for 15 minutes each night. During those phone calls we laughed, cried, and prayed together. It wasn't like being together, but it was still a bright moment in each day. He was working through a leveled system at the facility, and even though it was hard for him to do the right thing, he persevered. He had good days and bad. He ran away at one point and lost his shoes as a result. We were sad to hear he was acting out there, but we were also relieved that he was getting the chance to work through some of his struggles with 24-hour care surrounding him.

On our first off-campus visit with Alexander, we loaded the van with snacks and traveled to the dunes at Lake Michigan. We spent a wonderful carefree day at the beach. Alex allowed his newfound vocabulary of four letter words to sprinkle the day, but even when we confronted him, he was apologetic and respectful. We were so surprised.

After the beach, we decided to grab some ice cream at a local shop. We spoiled the kids a little, and everyone entered the car with a huge, dripping ice cream cone of their choosing. It was glorious, until we turned down the road toward the facility. We all felt uneasy as the sorrow engulfed us. Alexander began to plead with us not to take him back, but we stood firm, reminding him that he needed to get help so that our whole family could remain safe. He threw his seat belt off and tossed his ice cream cone onto the floor. He immediately started growling and crawled under the seat. We coaxed and encouraged him to come out, but I had started crying and my voice was not convincing him. Mike called the staff and told them we were about to pull into the parking lot with a very upset son.

I crawled down on the floor with him and tried to keep my voice calm. I wanted him to know how much we loved him and how much we wanted him back. I knew the words were a contradiction, but my heart felt convicted. He had just reminded all of us why he was there. The entire mood of the day was changed with an action by Alex. This was understandable, but his behavior at home had been like this for much smaller frustrations. I knew that we couldn't keep any of us safe if he came home like that, and so Mike and I stood firm. The staff knocked on the door while I still laid on the floor. Mike unlocked the door and they opened the side doors cautiously. I was relieved that they seemed to understand that this was defiance born out of anxiety, not a desire to hurt. The staff was firm but kind. They told him that his mom and dad loved him very much, but that he had to finish the program so that he could learn how to stay safe at home. He eventually climbed from under the seat and out of the van door. He walked between the staff members and never once looked back.

We were heartbroken, but we began to heal as a family despite the absence of one of our members. That summer we went to the pool, the park, and on a small vacation. It was incredible to see our other children invite friends over without fear of their brother's potential meltdown. They slowly began to relax while watching TV and in the car. They began to expect safety in their own home. It was so difficult for Mike and I to reconcile the feelings of freedom and utter loss. We missed him so much, but we were able to breathe in a way we hadn't been able to in years. He completed that program in October. Mike stayed home with the kids while I traveled to retrieve him.

We brought him home on Halloween day, just in time for our annual costume party. We had over invited as always. The entire neighborhood was in attendance as well as some of our former foster children and their families. We invited our parents as well as our close family friends. Everyone was thrilled to see Alexander. I could not take my eyes off him. I was filled with joy to have him home. It felt like our family was complete and I could not believe our fortune. We celebrated until late that night and everyone slept in the next morning, including Alexander. He was peaceful and cooperative for exactly two days.

His first meltdown was over being told that there was not enough time to ride his bike. He threw the bike at me and screamed a stream of curse words that would have impressed the crudest sailor. I let it go. The next day, he threw three loads of clean laundry down the basement stairs, and I calmly walked him through the coping skills we had just learned. We made posters that evening and hung them in the kitchen so that all of us could remember the skills we learned. That night at dinner he proudly shared them with everyone. Mike and I were proud of his enthusiasm and also of the other children for listening to him respectfully.

Alexander continued his roller coaster of behaviors for two more years. He was smart, funny, kind, impulsive, aggressive, caring, loving, deceitful, angry, and still our son. We loved him and refused to admit defeat. We willed him to act appropriately. We enlisted every resource we could find. He qualified for a wonderful program through our state which provided him with a therapist, habilitation provider, parent coach, and some weekends of respite. It was a lot of work to keep up with the program, but it was also really good for him to have so many people around him who loved and cared for him.

Our wraparound caseworker helped us to get creative with the resources that had been provided. We were able to place cameras in our home so that Alexander could have the freedom of being in a room alone while still having supervision. The following year we received funds again through the program, and we were able to use them to pay for obedience training for our dachshund, Gretchen. The first few weeks of training went really well. Alex loved learning how to teach our dog. He listened to the instructor and tried to be diligent with the training even when we came home. We were so proud and thrilled that he was using his energy in a positive way.

On the third week Alexander was agitated during the drive to training. He refused to stay in his seat and began grabbing for the steering wheel. I begged him to stop. Joelle and Camille were tagging along that night to see all the progress Gretchen and Alexander had made. Joelle was in the front seat and Camille was buckled into the seat next to Alex. He lunged at her and I could see the action in the rearview mirror. I quickly pulled off to the side of the road and put the car in park. "Alexander, you need to stop this right now. I need you to stop please." I tried to stay calm, but my heart was beginning to pound in my chest. "I need you to stop. Your therapist told us that it was time to call the police if you can't keep yourself or others safe. You need to be buckled and you need to keep your hands off your sister." Alexander's eyes were wide and his breathing was shallow and rapid.

"Just call them," Joelle said without expression. "Seriously, Mom, it's time to stop threatening." I knew she was right, but my hand still shook while I dialed the number. Alexander grabbed Joelle's seatbelt and began pulling it against her throat. I climbed directly into the back seat and put him into a hold while my phone was sitting on the center console.

I had almost forgotten that I made the call, but the operator picked up on the second ring. I explained the situation to her as I motioned for the girls to step out of the car. Alexander was flailing like a fish out of water and I began to get worried that the likelihood of him hurting someone by mistake was nearly as possible as him hurting someone on purpose. The officer approached the car casually. By the time he arrived, Alex was sitting in his seat with his arms folded, Joelle and Camille were standing near the ditch on the side of the road, and I was sitting next to Alex in the back seat.

I exited the car while still explaining to Alex what was happening. "I'm going to talk to the police now. They need to talk with you about safety." I got out of the car, but stood next to Alexander's door. The officer began to lecture me about the importance of requiring my children to stay in the seat belt. He told me that if I would just discipline him properly, I would not have this problem. He assured me that he and his wife have three children and they had never had a problem like this because they just tell their kids that they have to stay in their seats.

I tried to explain that my son has a traumatic brain injury caused by drug and alcohol exposure before birth. He smirked at me and I felt my blood begin to boil. He turned away from me and opened the car door and began to talk in a friendly cartoon-like voice to my son. Before he was done with his reminder of the importance of wearing a seat belt, he scooped Alexander up and placed him on the hood of the police car where he produced a sticker and stuck it to the front of my son's snot-covered t-shirt. I was furious, but I had discovered that the police would not be of any help that day. I put all three of my children back into the car and drove away.

We went to dog training that week, but I did not celebrate the success and neither did Joelle and Camille. I vowed to write a letter to the police station the next day. I didn't though because I realized it was going to take a little more than 12 hours to calm down. I did write the letter a week later, just in time for another call to the police. I didn't want to make the call, but Alex refused to get on the bus in the morning and when he finally did, he kicked the bus driver. The aide on the bus called me as the bus made a circle around the block and deposited him directly back onto my lawn.

I brought him inside after apologizing to the bus driver. He didn't want to hear my correction, and when I told him to get in the car to go to school, he lunged at me and grabbed for my throat. I was shocked and almost fell over. I reached behind me and unlocked my phone with one hand while trying to pry his fingers from my face with the other. I successfully dialed the number to his therapist who picked up on the first ring. She could hear the screaming in the background and immediately asked if she should call the police. That's when I lost my cool. I put the phone on speaker and moved Alexander to a safe hold. He continued to bite at me and thrash his body, but I haltingly told the story of the previous run-in with police the week prior. She agreed to put me on hold and make the call herself.

Within moments, the police officer showed up and came through the front door where we were sitting in a tangled mess. Alexander looked up at the officer and stopped immediately. One officer took him into the dining room to talk and the other officer kept me in the hallway. I launched into the same story I had told a million times. I overheard the first officer telling Alexander that he needed to stop strangling his mom. I could barely stop myself from rolling my eyes. The officers left, and I drove Alex to school.

When we arrived, he refused to get out of the car again. I was exhausted and defeated. I tried to speak calmly to him, but his eyes were glazed over and blank. He flew from his seat into mine and put his foot on the horn. I grasped his knee and tried to bend it away from the steering wheel. His body was everywhere and he did not seem to have the ability to stop. I didn't want the police to be there so I called my friend Nicole, who I knew was close by, and then I reluctantly called Mike. Things had been rocky at his new job, and I hesitated before I called his number. I knew he was under the gun and I feared that he would lose his job if he came to rescue me.

I called anyway. My friend pulled into the parking lot and walked cautiously to my door. She asked how she could help and I started to cry.

"It's okay. It's really okay. We are going to figure out what to do together," she assured me. I pulled Alexander to the floor of the car and wrapped my body around him as I handed Nicole the keys. She began to drive. "Where do you want me to go?" she asked gently.

"Back to the psych ward," I replied. Mike met us in the parking lot of the hospital. Nicole offered to wait, but I wanted to be alone with my mess and she graciously understood. Alexander was as exhausted and defeated as I was. He had fought relentlessly the entire way to the hospital.

I braced myself for the inevitable chase that would follow the opening of the van door. To my surprise, Alexander entered the building on his own and walked directly to the registration desk. Mike and I followed closely behind. The receptionist took one look at me and her eyes widened. "Right this way," she said bypassing the waiting room. She led us down a long corridor and into a room with furniture bolted to the floor. "If you want to clean up, there is a restroom right over here," her tone was sympathetic. I was surprised by her reaction until I observed my own face in the distorted reflection of the safety mirror. A large bruise was swelling on my cheek. Blood trickled down both arms where scratch marks were visible. My hair was sticking straight out at the side; the ends were broken and frayed. I turned the faucet to cold, never taking my eyes off my reflection. I scrubbed at the dried blood, and smoothed out my hair. I dried my hands and promised myself I wouldn't forget what this moment felt like. I wouldn't cover up my fear. I would not live this way anymore.

# CHAPTER 18

# Psychiatric Ward

Alexander spent the next ten days in the adolescent psychiatric ward. He made no improvement, and after a careful review of all the medications that had been tried in the past, everyone felt that medication was also not the answer. The social worker sat with us for the second time and recommended residential treatment. Mike was worn thin and the exhaustion of the last ten years was etched onto his face. I sat next to him on the small plastic love seat and the social worker sat in a chair just to the right of me. Our knees could almost touch in her tiny office.

She placed a stack of informational packets on the coffee table between us. "I can't recommend a place but these are the facilities that have openings at this time." The weight of failure pressed in around me. I had desperately tried to avoid this exact outcome. Tears were brimming in my eyes and the brochures blurred before me. I knew I needed to be present for this decision but I was desperately fighting the urge to run. I placed my hands on each of my knees pushing them toward the floor, willing them to stay put. I pictured myself jumping up from the couch, flinging the door open and grabbing my son. I imagined that I would put my hand in Alexander's and run away with him that very moment. We could just start over like none of this had ever happened.

Then I remembered that I was locked behind three steel doors, that Alex was waiting in the next room wearing sweatpants with the drawstring removed, a white undershirt, and a pair of no-slip socks. He wasn't even dressed to leave the building. This predicament was a result of his dangerous behavior. No amount of running would find us a solution. I tuned back into the conversation to hear my husband asking questions about each facility. We knew we couldn't take him home, so without much conviction, we pointed to a flyer. "This one," I said, and my heart broke a little more for my son.

Alexander lasted seven months at the program. Each day he was worse than when he started. He refused to do any schoolwork and insisted on fighting with anyone who dared look his way. He would not comb or cut his hair, and absolutely rejected the idea of bathing or brushing his teeth properly. He had a therapist that took away visits and phone calls as a punishment. We could not convince her that his childhood neglect and abuse made it impossible for him to see the punishment as temporary. As soon as his phone calls were removed, Alex's behavior escalated. When his visits were also removed, he shut down completely. We tried to comply with the standard of the facility but became increasingly worried.

He was kicked out on a Thursday. He had broken a staff member's leg while trying to escape his locked-down facility. I received the call on a chilly October morning. "Ma'am, we can't keep him anymore. We will need you to come and sign the discharge papers." I sat silent on the other end. "Ma'am?"

I felt the anger rising from the core of my being. "If you can't handle him, what am I supposed to do? I have five other children living at home. What if he hurts one of them? What if he kills someone? I'm not being dramatic here, that's what you're worried about too right? I love him more than I can express, but how is this safe?"

Another pause in the conversation and then, "I don't know what to tell you. We will keep him for a few more days until you make a plan. Maybe try the state hospital." I shouted back, losing all control of my voice, "I already did — his IQ is one point too low — ONE POINT! No one will help us." My voice trailed off as I realized the speaker on the other end didn't care. I knew they were fed up with his antics, but what was I supposed to do? I hung up without saying goodbye.

I picked him up on a Monday morning and I refused to sign any of the discharge paperwork. I wanted him out of that place as badly as he wanted out, but I refused to say that it was my choice. I missed him desperately, but I was afraid of him. I was afraid of what he might do in our home.

We brought him home just before Thanksgiving. I had spent my week calling every place in the country asking for someone who could help a child with an IQ of 69, Fetal Alcohol Spectrum Disorder, Attachment Disorder, and a tendency toward violence. We were shut down at every turn until I called Teen Challenge. They had one place that would take a child as young as 11. They were willing to talk as a staff, do some research, and, most importantly, they were willing to pray. They promised they would take the next 48 hours to commit our son to prayer.

When they called back to offer him a place, I was shocked. I hadn't thought that they would actually say yes. I had committed that same 48 hours to prayer though, and Mike and I had enlisted our close friends and family as well. I knew I shouldn't actually be surprised that the Lord had provided. I knew He loved my son more than I ever could.

We sat down with Alexander the next day and explained the new plan. He was sad but understood that he needed a different environment to learn and grow. We prayed together as a family and celebrated a tearful Thanksgiving together before traveling the nine hours to his new home.

They were very strict on their intake procedure. We pulled into the gravel parking lot and were immediately met by three staff members and two older residents. They shook our hands warmly and turned immediately to Alexander. They required him to look them in the eyes and stand up straight. They were firm with him, but also kind and respectful. I fought back tears, but the peace in my heart was undeniable. I knew we had chosen the right place for our son. The cost for the program was high, but I had never been more sure that our financial sacrifice was worth it.

The staff took Alexander and gave him a haircut, a tour of the facility, and the uniform he would wear for the next 15 months. We hugged and kissed goodbye. We waved goodbye as we wound back down the driveway until we could no longer see our son.

The car ride home was heavy with sorrow and loss but also slightly lightened by the hope that our son would soon find the strength and the will to change.

Mike and I set about the work of once again bringing healing to our home. In August we received a phone call at 3:00 a.m. I grabbed the phone and held it up to my eyes, squinting to see the number without my glasses. It was Teen Challenge. My heart sank as I answered the call. The director's voice was even and serious. He informed me that Alexander had been in a fight earlier. The fight was mutual but the other boy sustained a broken collarbone. Alexander had reacted by screaming and yelling for hours at the top of his lungs. He was throwing things on the floor and eventually had to be restrained. I could hear the director's voice shake as he told the story. They had tried so hard to help Alexander and I knew how devastating it could feel to constantly put forth the effort only to see this child regress.

Mike woke up as I was talking, and I quickly put the phone on speaker. We both listened and encouraged the staff. We were terrified that the other family might sue us, but there was nothing we could do about it that night. I hung up the phone and pressed my face to my pillow. Mike tried to calm me down, but the waves of sobs came one after another. I could not find the words to pray. I tried but nothing came. I remembered that the Holy Spirit would intercede for me, and I allowed it. I allowed my own mind to let go. I finally fell asleep from complete exhaustion.

Alexander lasted another two months at Teen Challenge. They tried everything to re-engage him, but he had completely shut down. They prayed and talked with us. I wanted to be angry. I wanted to believe they were giving up on him, but I knew my son too well to believe that. I knew he pushed every good thing away. We worked with Teen Challenge to find a safe place for Alexander to finish out the 15 months of his program. We all hoped a change of scenery would give Alex a fresh start. It didn't. He stayed two months at the next program before we conceded that he was not in a good place. We brought him home just in time for another Thanksgiving.

Alexander was a dream to live with for three weeks. He was kind to his brothers, helpful around the house, and fun to talk to. He worked hard at school and his teacher loved him. In January he made a friend who liked to set fires, sneak out, and steal things. Before we knew what was happening, Alexander was doing things I didn't ever dream he would do. The more we protested the friendship the harder he pursued it. Alexander was increasingly agitated and impulsive.

One night after we tucked him into bed, I went into the kitchen to finish dishes. Mike ran to the store to gather meal items for the following day. We had become accustomed to shopping each day in an effort to curb some of Alexander's food hoarding. We had let the dishes go for the entire day, and I sighed at the amount I would have to complete. I dialed my mom's number and settled in for a good chat as I worked. I hung up just as Mike pulled into the driveway. It had turned out to be perfect timing. After putting the groceries away and packing lunches for the following day, we retreated to the family room to watch a show.

We were settled in, quietly laughing when my phone received a text message. I was confused by the number. I opened the message to find that it was the mom of Alexander's friend. She was asking how late Alexander was allowed to stay. I flew off the couch and into our son's bedroom. He wasn't there. I looked all through the house and finally found a window in the hallway just slightly cracked. I returned to the family room fuming. Mike and I agreed to pretend to go to bed and send a text back to the mother. We asked her to send him home and then shut off every light and locked all the doors and windows.

We watched from a second-story window as Alex came around the block and crossed our street. He came around the side of the house and tried each window. When he couldn't get inside, he pulled the trash can to a low hanging part of the roof. We couldn't believe it. He began to try to jimmy a second-story window just as we made ourselves known. We told him to get off the roof and opened the back door to let him in. He told a few stories that had no substance and finally retreated to his bedroom. For the next month, Mike and I took turns sleeping outside of his door to make sure he was safe. He gave up the friend in April, but the sneaky behavior did not stop completely. It was becoming increasingly difficult to keep him safe once again.

## Thirteen-Year-Old Tantrum

I found myself weeping with my fists pressed tightly to my eyeballs. It was the kind of ugly crying that causes the one doing the crying to suck in loud, ragged breaths. I was lamenting the lack of pastries at our local coffee shop. I had arrived just as the last apple crumble coffee cake left the rack in the hands of a greedy stranger. I didn't really know if she was greedy, but I felt angry at her nonetheless. She didn't know what kind of weekend I had. She might have handed me that last slice if she had only known. I watched her walk to her seat and take a bite of the gooey goodness and I secretly hoped the confection was as dry as the desert. It wasn't. I could tell by her mocking smile as she took a second bite.

I stepped toward the cashier and ordered a small cup of coffee. I knew I would have to settle. I turned to fill my mug and read the chalkboard labels above each carafe carefully. Hazelnut. I liked hazelnut the best. I placed my cup carefully under the spout and pulled the lever toward me. Coffee grounds sloshed into the bottom of my cup. Empty.

That was the theme of my day. Emptiness. I felt like someone drained me like a decanter of stale coffee. I wasn't just running low; I was empty. Not empty enough to be free from tears I discovered too late. I set the empty mug next to the empty pot just as the tears began to fill my lids and overflow. I tried not to make eye contact with the other customers as I fled to the parking lot. My messenger bag felt heavy as I pulled the door I was supposed to push. The strap of the bag caught on the handle, and as I detangled it from the door, the tears spilled over, splashing next to my feet.

A man tried to pass me in the entrance and stopped to ask, "Are you okay, ma'am?"

A small part of me felt thankful that he asked and the rest of me felt humiliated. "Um, oh yes, I'm okay. I just have something in my contact." He looked directly at the glasses perched on the end of my nose. Realizing my mistake, I ducked my head and darted for my car.

I sat in the car for a long time. I let the tears fall and the blotchy patches form on my pale skin. I knew my eyes were getting puffy, but I didn't even try to stop. I wiped my nose with a crumpled up fast-food napkin. A few folks walked past and peered into my window. I was grateful as each one turned their eyes away pretending not to see the grown woman weeping. Once there wasn't a tear left to shed, I sat in silence for a while, soaking up the quiet of the car. The weight of loneliness and isolation pressing in on me, I allowed myself to just feel it. This life hadn't turned out the way I had hoped, and I grieved. I mourned the loss of the teenager I thought I would raise. Our son kept us in solitude most days. We spent hyper-vigilant days chasing after him and sleepless nights on a chair outside his door in fear that we would wake up the next morning to find him gone.

Alexander was 13 at the time. He had become a walking con-tradiction. One day compassionate, patient, and kind and the next day hateful, impulsive, and dangerous. By the time he turned 13 he had been detained by the police three times and reported for battery seven times. He slid by each time, facing little to no consequence. I woke each day tiptoeing through my routine in hopes of preventing the unstable relationship from cracking. The worst was when one of us went out of town or had to work late. If we served at church, he would become edgy. If one of the other kids had a birthday party or play date he would sabotage any chance of joy. He pouted and sulked if we didn't give him our undivided attention, but if anyone else wanted a little of our time he groaned, kicked, or whispered threats to the other children.

The weekend before my own meltdown was filled with a series of 13-year-old meltdowns. It began when he felt too tired to go to football practice. He called from school asking me to pick him up because he had a headache. I always wanted to believe him, but there was a part of me that questioned the validity of his excuse. I picked him up anyway and immediately had to stop at the library. He was surprisingly helpful at finding the books I was looking for.

He asked to spend his lawn mowing money to buy both of us a treat. I was shocked. I agreed, and we each got a pastry. The afternoon was shaping up to be a good one. There was no evidence of a splitting headache, but I was content to give him what seemed to be a much-needed hour of extra attention. He smiled at me and told me funny stories from his day. He shared all the things he loved about football and listened as I told him stories about my job. I let my guard down. I wanted the mother and son relationship with this first precious son of mine more than I could describe. I genuinely felt at peace as I pulled into the driveway. It was raining and we laughed as we darted from the car to the front door squealing at the cool autumn shower.

As soon as we threw the door open, the mood shifted. The other children had arrived home while we were out. I shook off my wet hair and reached out to hug each of them. That's when I noticed Alexander's face had changed. He was sticking his tongue out at his youngest brother. Sage never could ignore, and immediately began to scream in protest.

"Ignore him. Please just ignore him. I want to see you. Don't let that ruin your night," I pleaded. It was too late. Alexander grabbed Sage's Lego creation and broke the top off of it. "No!" I wheeled around and looked straight at Alex. "No! I mean it. Put that down.

He didn't do anything to you. We just had such a good afternoon. Please don't ruin it now." Sage shed large tears and balled his fists up tightly. Our night was quickly heading toward disaster and it was only 4:00. "Please go to your room and cool off Alexander. Just take five minutes."

His face was fierce. "No. No. You can't make me. I'm not going to do it," he replied. I firmly restated the direction but his response was the same. "Nope. I hate you. I'm not going. All you care about is the little baby. You only care about everyone but me." He swore loudly and I felt my temperature rising.

I firmly repeated the direction once again. "Go to your room. You need to cool off, and so do we."

He crossed his arms and made no move to obey. Finally, he turned to me and said, "If it wasn't against the law, I'd punch him in his little baby face."

I put myself between Alexander and the other children and said firmly, "Safety plan." *Safety plan* is our cue to the other children to get to a safe place. We will not allow threatening behavior or words. Camille and Joelle glared at Alexander as they got up off the couch, shut the TV off, and gathered their brothers.

Joelle looked at the little ones and sighed. She forced her voice to sound upbeat, "Well, what should we do? Do you want to go for a walk, jump on the trampoline, or pick a movie to watch upstairs?" We added a second television to our home the summer Alexander was 13 because he would often stand in front of the television during a tantrum. We wanted the other kids to have something to do when Alexander's outbursts took up too much time.

"I'm not going anywhere!" Jude shouted with an unexpected firmness. "Alexander ruins everything. I hate the safety plan. I hate him!"

Keeping one eye on Alexander, I crouched down next to Jude, "I know you're mad. You have every right to be. I need you to be safe now though. When daddy gets home, I'll take you to do something special, okay?" He stuck his tongue out at his brother and reluctantly followed the girls into the other room. Camille took his hand and led him to the dining room.

Joelle asked again, "What should we do, guys?" They chose to watch a movie and headed for the upstairs. I heard the lock click on the door at the bottom of the steps and I knew they would also lock the one to our room as well. That was the rule: locked doors, stay together, stay safe.

Alexander continued his tantrum for about 15 minutes, which wasn't too long. When he finished, his body became less tense and his eyes began to focus again. Eventually he made eye contact and said, "I'm sorry, Mom. What can I do to pay you back for your time?"

I took a deep breath. I wanted to forgive, but I felt the pull of my heart toward my other children who still hid behind two locked doors. I knew that no one should have to live that way, and it tore me into pieces. I said, "I forgive you," with less enthusiasm than I would have liked. "I need you to give everyone an hour of peace. I need you to sit in your room with the door shut and allow everyone to have peace."

He whipped around and shouted. "I don't care what they need. They're a bunch of little babies. I don't care what you want."

I sighed, feeling myself losing the ability to see the good in my firstborn son. I sat on a chair in the dining room pretending not to care. "That's fine, take all the time you need. You owe us some peace. The hour will start when you go in your room and shut the door," I said firmly.

I knew I was losing the strength to keep my cool and began to pray out loud. "Lord, I need You right now. Alexander needs You too. He needs to know he has been created by You with a purpose to do so much more than scare others and throw tantrums. I'm asking that Jesus will be present in Alexander's life. I pray that Satan will leave him alone. I ask that Your Holy Spirit will fill this place and fill the emptiness in Alexander's heart."

As I prayed, Alex began to pace in front of me mumbling, "Shut up, shut up, shut up, shut up."

I prayed louder, "Lord, Alexander needs You more than ever. He was hurt when he was a baby, but You love him and I love him. His Daddy loves him and his brothers and sisters love him too. Please Lord, take hold of his heart and fill it with Your peace."

I could see his composure changing, and I continued to pray. He walked toward me and placed his hand on my knee. "Amen," he whispered.

"Amen," I said.

Alexander took his hour in his room and then mowed the lawn without complaint. He took his shower and helped with the dishes. The rest of the night was great until bedtime. He started the disrespectful refusal again. The next morning the cycle repeated. Tantrum, safety plan, repentance. Then repeated again in the afternoon. Tantrum, safety plan, repentance. Then repeated again in the evening. Tantrum, safety plan, repentance. Then repeated three more times Sunday. By the time Monday rolled around, I felt defeated, lonely, isolated, and weary and so I wept. I sobbed over the pastry because the truth of my son's brokenness and my own was so much more than I could bear.

## CHAPTER 19

# Depression

Sometimes I embodied the mental illness more than my son. At least that's the way it seemed. Weekends were the worst for me. In my mind I always played up the possibilities, but the reality of a Saturday with nothing to do loomed largely in my subconscious. Other families were excited at the prospect of a three-day weekend. "I could sure use a three-day vacation." Or, "This weekend is going to be just what my family needs. Three days off from school. My kids are going to be so happy. How about you?"

That was the point in the conversation where I had to choose the lie or the truth. The lie would be "Yes! Absolutely, I can't wait for the three-day weekend. I'm going to have so much fun with my kids." The truth: "A long weekend feels like a prison sentence. My son will tantrum at least five times each day. We will have to turn down invitations to cookouts, bonfires, and trips to the park." The even more depressing truth: "We won't be invited anywhere anyway." I chose to just nod at those who saw the weekend as a blessing instead of a curse. Inside, my heart felt the weight of the reality that always seemed to come.

The sun pierced the darkening shade I had hung in my room the week previous. It was the first Saturday that our family had nothing planned. Nothing at all. I reached around the still-sleeping body of my seven-year-old. I pulled at the corner of the shade and looked out at the yard. The sun was brilliant. The breeze fluttered through the open window. The cool, crisp morning indicated the coming fall. The smell was fresh and filled with hopeful promise.

Sage had his head pressed against Mike's pillow. I could barely remember him getting into our bed around 2:00 a.m. His nightmares had been the cause of many restless nights for both of us. He would stumble into our room at least five nights a week. Sometime he would grab the mat from under the bed and fix himself a place to sleep next to my side of the bed. If he was feeling especially needy he would grab a blanket from the foot of the bed and climb in the bed. If he curled up between our feet it left him plenty of room to spread out and even bring his own pillow, blanket, and stuffed animals. Sage always had trouble sleeping through the night. We kept an extra bed for him in our room from the time he was an infant. I closed the curtain and pulled Sage close to me. My heart ached for him. I don't know what thoughts swirled in his head, but I was glad he found peace with us nearby.

I put my head back on the pillow and thought of all the things we could do with this carefree day. Maybe a trip to the city? We could pick apples at the local farm. We could build that playhouse we had been planning for so many years. Maybe we could find a place to go swimming. The sun beckoned and my heart felt light and full of possibility. I had heard of a castle in Ohio. That would be a fun day trip! We could take a picnic. The new playground just opened in the neighboring town. I know the kids would love it. For a moment, I thought of the adventures we could have.

I heard the other children stirring downstairs. They would be getting dressed and fixing breakfast. Mike is an early riser, so I knew there was sure to be coffee. I tucked the blanket around Sage and tiptoed down the stairs. Before my feet hit the last step, I heard it. Alexander's voice, high-pitched, shouting above everyone. "I hate this family. I hate all of you. If I could punch you in the head, I would. I would. You know I would, and you can't stop me. You can't. I don't care."

I paused. My legs suddenly felt as if they had been filled with bags of sand. I could hear Mike's low voice, reasoning and trying to calm him. Each sentence was met by Alexander's response, "I don't care." I took a deep breath. I knew I needed to give Mike a break. I stood up, but my body felt heavy.

"What's going on?" I said, as I took in the scene. The little boys were scooping cereal into their mouths mechanically, staring out the window. Camille had headphones on, listening to music too loudly. I could hear the beat across the room. Joelle had her nose in a book, looking oblivious to the drama. I knew that was far from the truth. She observed everything. She remembered everything. I noticed she was tense in her seat, ready to jump up at any moment.

I stood between the kids and Alexander. "I don't want to talk about this here. Please step into your room or on the porch. You are scaring the other kids," I ordered with a calm that didn't quite match my actual racing heart.

"I don't care," he responded with pupils dilated and wrinkled forehead.

"I understand that. You will be grounded to the property today if you threaten anyone else. I'm stepping back. Daddy is away from you too. No one is hurting you. You are not allowed to hurt anyone either. Please go to your room or the porch and calm down."

Mike nodded and both of us stood with hands raised in our most non-threatening pose. "See," he said, "no one is touching you. It's time for you to calm down and allow the other kids to calm down too."

Alexander opened his mouth and then closed it again. He turned and shouted one more time, "You are the worst family. I hate all of you." Then he went into his room and slammed the door.

Mike and I sat with the kids at the table and struck up a non-related subject. "How did everyone sleep?"

They all half smiled. "Okay."

I tried to talk myself out of the inevitable depression that was already developing. It starts in my mind. It's almost an audible voice telling me that I'm a failure. My children aren't ever going to be okay. I work too much. I'm too anxious all the time. I should lose weight, work out more, eat healthier, have more fun, work harder. The words don't have to make sense or even be a consistent thought. Next I feel a heaviness in my chest and a pressure on my shoulders. All of my brilliant plans begin to burst like soap bubbles. Short-lived sweet dreams that never amount to anything.

I could see the weight on my children as well. I knew they were struggling with the realization that they were facing three days of being trapped with a brother who was never happy and always on edge. They knew that the weekend would be a roller coaster of emotions. They knew it and so did I. The sun still streamed in through the open window, but when my eight-year-old asked to watch TV, I agreed.

Alexander had calmed and willingly gone to his room, but we would need to wait out the emotional stabilization that typically takes an hour. I turned the TV to a cartoon and felt the weight of hopelessness take hold. I curled up next to the kids and read a book for a while. I put the book down and napped until I heard Alexander open his door. "Hey, Mom, I'm sorry."

I looked up at him, "I know. I accept your apology." I did. I was telling the truth, but the weight didn't lift with the words. I drug myself off the couch and began to fix an early lunch.

Sage played with Legos in the kitchen while I worked. Alexander walked past and knocked them all on the floor. When Sage started to cry, Alexander responded, "Why don't you cry, baby?" I sent him to his room. He stayed ten minutes, and when the timer went off, he apologized.

Alexander pulled all of the tools out of the shed and spread them over the backyard. Mike caught him trying to break the fence with an ax. When he asked what was going on, Alexander replied. "Oh, my gosh! You never let me do anything. I just want wood for the campfire." He yelled at Mike and then took ten minutes to cool off in his room. We set the timer, and when it went off, he apologized.

The girls were making bracelets in the family room while our kitten Cleo scampered among the supplies scattering them everywhere. When Alexander walked into the room, he exclaimed, "You guys are such idiots. The cat is getting into everything. She's going to die if she eats any of that stuff." Before they could answer, he continued, "Fine, if you don't care. I guess she's just going to die. You don't even care. You're killing her. Don't cry to me when she dies." Joelle looked up in anger.

I sent him to his room again. He refused to go and slammed furniture around the room for a few minutes, then went to his room and slammed the door. When he was calm, he came out and apologized.

Late in the afternoon, we decided to try the park. We had all been pretty excited about the possibility of a new park adventure, but the excitement was tempered by the reality that sometimes Alexander had trouble riding in the car. We arranged seats so that Alexander sat away from the other children.

Mike and I talked with excitement and listened to the little boys chatter, but our emotions clearly didn't match our words. Our hyper-vigilance was noticed by Alexander who took offense. "Why do you always have to watch me? Why do you treat me like a baby? I'm 13!"

I looked at him as he sat in the front seat and snapped, "We have to treat you like a baby because you act like a baby. You can't even sit in the backseat with your brothers because we don't trust you." I knew that the words hurt him, but I also needed him to see the toll his actions were taking. Snapping at him never accomplished anything, and it didn't that time either. He cussed under his breath, and I folded my arms and looked out the window at the passing cars. We made the rest of the trip in silence.

We arrived at the park, and the boys unloaded their bikes. They were excited to go on new trails, and they were antsy to get going. Alexander jumped out of the front seat and began unloading the bikes. He talked with kindness and gentleness. "Hey, buddy, don't worry. I'll get your bike for you. Hang on just a second. Here you go."

I still felt angry, but Alex had switched gears again. It was good to see him treat his brothers with respect, but it made my head spin. I still felt frustrated, but he was trying to make things right. We had come to know that the FASD brain cycles from one emotion to another with extreme impulsivity and little thought for those around who may suffer the consequences of living with a person in constant mood swings.

I laughed and talked with the kids while we rode bikes, skipped stones in the lake, and explored the park with excitement. I did begin to feel a little better, but I was tired from standing between Alexander and his brothers. I felt a constant need to protect. I couldn't look away for even a moment. The park was a success, and even the drive home was pleasant.

When I began to fix a snack upon the return home, Alexander's temper flared again. "Sage looked at me, and Ezra keeps smiling. Just look at him. I hate them. They never get in trouble. You just care about them! I'm going to run away."

We hadn't been home three minutes. I'd only had time to put peanut butter on one slice of bread. I couldn't even complete a PB&J sandwich properly. The darkness and loss of hope began closing in on me. I set the knife down and asked Mike to keep an eye on the boys. I had to get out of there. I walked toward the driveway and realized I had lost the will to even go anywhere.

I climbed the stairs to my room and climbed under the covers. The little boys brought blankets and books and read quietly while I pretended to sleep, wiping tears silently. I hoped that Mike was supervising Alexander, but I didn't care as long as the other kids were safe. I felt horrible for feeling the way I was toward my own son. I felt blank and tired and emotionless. I felt like no mother at all. This isn't the way I planned my life. I planned love and adventure and joy. The joy was gone. I put the pillow over my head and pressed my hands to my ears. I wished for all of it to go away. I wished for my life to go away. I was certain that God had made a mistake. I wasn't the one he meant to raise these children. He couldn't have possibly entrusted me with them. I was just messing it up one day at a time. Every day felt worse than the last.

Depression ruled the rest of my day. I forced myself to try to make the day good for the rest of the kids but I couldn't shake the miserable feelings. When they were finally tucked into bed. Alexander made three more appearances to tell us that we never let him use the bathroom, get a drink, or have a snack. Finally, he fell asleep and I crashed on the couch to watch TV. I couldn't concentrate though. I couldn't cry, laugh, or yell. Mike and I just sat there together, feeling emotionally beaten.

"I hope tomorrow's better," I said.

"Me too," he nodded. Then I realized I hadn't lost complete hope. Tomorrow would be a new day. Depression wouldn't have the last word on that day.

# CHAPTER 20

# Just a Normal Kid

Alexander's obsessive behavior had taken a new form the spring he turned 13. He decided that he loved football. He loved everything about football. He begged to watch online videos of players making impossible touchdowns. He practiced his touchdown dance in the family room and at one point even cleaned his cleats over my brand new carpet. He wore his football gloves to toss the ball and to ride his bike. He refused to take off his Ohio State jersey even after wearing it for three days in a row. I soon became weary of the constant conversation about cleats, football gloves, and jerseys. What was once a healthy interest was quickly becoming an unhealthy obsession.

When he was outside playing with the neighbors, I would catch a glimpse of the friend he could be, but there was always an uncertainty, a teetering of emotions. One day as he and two other boys tossed the ball around, I could see Alexander becoming agitated. I was standing in the kitchen, finishing up the dinner dishes. I couldn't hear the conversation, but I knew enough of the mannerisms to know that things were about to blow up. I dropped the towel on the floor and flew to the door. I was running frantically through the grass when I saw Alexander grab his friend. With one hand on his neck and another on the collar of his shirt, Alexander threw him to the ground. The other child lay there for a moment, dazed. I stopped short of tripping over him and pointed at my son. "Get in the house now," I said in a low tone.

"I didn't do anything!" He screamed.

"I'll talk with you about it inside." I pointed to the house and reached a hand out to the friend who was now quickly wiping away a tear.

"I said I didn't do anything!" screamed Alexander.

I looked at the faces of the now-horrified neighbors. "I'm sorry that happened," I said. "It's time for you two to head home."

The boys walked off our property toward home, and I turned to face Alexander. He squared his shoulders to mine. Although he was still a few inches shorter than me, he looked me straight in the eye. "That kid's a baby. He's a little sissy. You never listen to me. I hate you. I'm not going inside. You can't make me."

I stood my ground and kept my hands where he could see them. "I watched the whole thing. You hurt him and he's your friend. I'm disappointed, but I'm not angry. It's time for you to go inside."

Alexander looked at the door and back at me and then in a growling voice, he strung together every curse word in the English language.

I took a deep breath as I responded. "I can't and won't make you go in the house, but I do hope that you make a good choice." I sidestepped him, sensing the steaming emotions still boiling off of him. I entered the house and picked up the towel and plate I had been drying when this all began. I looked around the house to make sure that all the other children were not in Alexander's path should he decide to come inside. They were playing quietly in their room with a bucket of blocks, so I peeked inside and said, "I'm just going to close the door for a few minutes. Alexander needs to cool off." They nodded and returned to their building.

Alexander stepped inside the mudroom and stood next to the door for a few moments. I knew not to engage at this point and went back to the dishes. After a few minutes, he began to attempt to engage me in the hateful conversation once again. I didn't bite. He paced, taking small steps, still standing by the back door. He tried again. This time he blamed me for never believing him. I still didn't take the bait. He tried to point a finger at his brothers, claiming that I loved them more than him. My blood started to boil, but I took a deep breath and wiped the counter down. As I finished sweeping the floor, he finally said. "I really didn't mean to hurt him. He just made me so mad."

I placed the broom back on the hook and sat down on the mudroom steps. Alexander was willing to finally talk, and I let him. It was difficult to allow him to work through all the steps of blaming and cursing and then owning his own decisions and then finally accepting his portion of the responsibility. He did it though and I was so relieved.

I sent him to the shower with instructions to bathe properly and brush his teeth. Once he was behind the locked door, I breathed deeply and sat down on the floor. It could have been so much worse, but it wasn't. I consciously filled and emptied my lungs slowly before rising to check on the little boys. When I opened their door, I found them still playing blocks and excited to show me the town they built. I crouched down next to them and thanked them for being patient while their big brother worked some emotions out. "It's okay, Momma. Is he okay now?" Ezra was always the first to make peace.

"Yes, he is. He's taking a shower now. Do you want to come pick out a movie we can all watch together tonight?"

"Yes!" they shouted. We chose a movie and settled in with a bowl of popcorn. When Alexander finally exited the bathroom he smelled great and I praised him. I invited him to watch the movie with us and he actually agreed without complaint. As he settled in next to me on the couch I felt surprised at how close he was sitting. It had been a long time since he wanted anything to do with me.

I was laughing along with the cartoon they had chosen when I noticed Alexander looking at me. "Are you okay?" I asked.

"It just, you know, um, I wish I could just be a normal kid. You know?" I did know. I hated to admit it even to myself. There were times I wished he could just be a normal kid too.

"You are a normal kid," I responded. "I know you lost your cool today but you turned it around and it didn't even take that long this time. Plus, you took a really good shower the first time I asked, and now you're watching a movie with your brothers. That seems pretty normal to me, don't you think?"

He paused for a moment. "Yeah, I guess you're right. I'm going to try harder though, Mom." I turned back to the movie before he could see me tear up. For that moment, life did feel pretty normal.

Alexander still had to take a consequence for hurting his friend. Mike and I settled on one week with no football and a humble apology to his friend. The next day, he refused to accept the consequence. He started into his one-sided dialogue about how the other kid was at fault and then he blamed our family for his choices. "This family is so stupid. God shouldn't have put me here; you guys are idiots."

I hadn't yet poured my morning coffee and I was already wishing I could go back to bed. I grabbed a warm mug and put it between my hands as I gathered my thoughts. "You know what, Alexander? You told me something last night that really stuck with me. Do you know what that was?"

His face was set with a hard expression, his mouth one thin line. "No," he grunted.

"Do you want to know?" I asked.

"I guess," he grunted again.

"You told me you want to be a normal kid. I want that for you too. Do you know what is normal? It's making mistakes and accepting the consequences. Even moms and dads have to accept consequences from time to time. Remember that speeding ticket I got last year?"

His expression still pinched at his face. Then he relaxed a little. "I remember," he said quietly.

"Well, I didn't want to pay for that ticket. I didn't mean to speed. I really didn't even want to break the law, but I did. I wasn't paying attention and there was a price to pay. It wasn't the end of the world though; it was just a ticket. This consequence isn't the end of the world either. It's just one week. Normal kids mess up, and then normal kids take their consequences." I sipped my coffee and waited for what I assumed was going to be a belligerent response. For the second day in a row, I found myself shocked.

"Okay," he said. I turned and walked into the other room and put the football back in the closet.

The truth about football is this — I don't like it. I grew up in Ohio, and I like the Ohio State Buckeyes because everyone likes the Buckeyes. It's something we are practically taught at birth. I watched as classmates joined the team and even went on to play pro. I was still pretty disinterested in the sport as a whole. I didn't like the idea of smashing into one another over something as silly as a ball. I didn't like the potential for broken bones and brain damage. I was relieved when my four daughters chose calm things like choir, band, and theater. I was not particularly thrilled when Alexander began to show interest in football. All I could think of was the pictures I'd seen of the drug- and alcohol-exposed brain. I knew that he was already struggling with difficulties, and I was terrified that he would end up with further complications. Not to mention the fact that other boys his age had always been bigger than he is and their one goal would be to slam him into the ground at full force. I envisioned myself unable to restrain my emotions and jumping the bleachers to take a brother out for hurting my baby boy. After the incident with the neighbor, I was also worried that Alexander might not be able to separate the aggression of the game with his tendency toward aggression in everyday situations.

Mike and Alexander and I had some heated discussions over the next few weeks. I was firmly against him joining the middle school team. Alexander was worried about not understanding or remembering the plays. He was also afraid to miss out on the opportunity to be on the team. Mike did a great job of staying neutral. We eventually decided to allow him to go to overnight football camp with the team. We all agreed that we would table the discussion until the end of camp. I was a complete wreck until the day Mike dropped him off. He called me as he left the college campus. "It was amazing. The coaches were great; the other kids were excited to see him. One even shouted across the campus and ran up to see him. Everyone was genuinely happy to see him." His voice cracked as he recounted the experience. I teared up as I listened. "He just looked, you know, normal."

I couldn't believe what I was hearing. My husband sounded as shocked and relieved as I felt. I picked my son up three days later, and I almost didn't recognize him. He jogged off the field and straight toward me, smiling. I followed him to his dorm room expecting a complete mess. Everything was already packed neatly into his suitcase and his room was as neat as a pin. We checked out and returned his key, which he shockingly hadn't lost. I spent the hour-long drive home sneaking glances at him. He just seemed so grown up, like a little man.

The following Saturday, his team played a round of scrimmages with local teams. I still wasn't sure about this whole football nonsense. I woke him up at 7:00 and expected him to refuse to get out of bed. He jumped right up and grabbed his football gear and a few slices of toast and met me in the car. I hadn't really thought he was going to go so I was still in my pajamas. I was a little embarrassed as I dropped him off at the field and promised to return with real clothes on.

The sun was already scorching at 10:00 a.m. Alexander had been on the football field since 7:30. As I walked up to the bleachers I could feel my anxiety rising. We aren't typically a sports family, and I was nervous about how I would fit in with the other parents. I don't know the first thing about football and had been hesitant to allow Alexander to join the team. I settled onto the metal bleachers and immediately began to sweat. Drops rolled from my forehead, and my own hair had become too hot to touch. I was impressed by all the boys on the field playing their hearts out without complaint.

"Berry, I love the aggression, but I really need you to bring it over here." My ears perked up. He was talking to my son. I chuckled a little. This was the one place Alexander's aggression might be a good thing.

I watched my son accept the correction with an attitude of respect. "Yes, sir," he responded. It was 98 degrees with 100 percent humidity, and for the first time all summer I was thankful for the miserable weather. The perspiration was indistinguishable from the tears that were now streaming. I wiped away the tears and the sweat and relished the moment. In this moment, he was just a normal kid.

## CHAPTER 21

# Arrested

"Safety plan!" I hollered as he rushed toward me. Joelle and Camille rose from the couch and motioned Ezra, Jude, and Sage toward the hallway. They moved slowly and I motioned for them to speed up. "Both doors locked," I reminded as his hands pressed to my throat. He looked me directly in the eyes. I marveled at how tall he had gotten. I should have been scared, but I was just exhausted. "Alexander, don't do this. You are going to hurt me." I kept my tone even as I worked my hands slowly toward his wrists.

"I don't care. I hope you die! I hate this family." We were so close I could see his pupils dilate till they seemed to swallow his iris.

"Dad's going to be home in a few minutes," I reminded. "I really don't want to call the police again. Remember what the officer told you? You can't keep doing this. You're a teenager now. You are going to get charged with a crime, and they won't keep letting me defend you."

He sneered, "I don't care about you. You hate me anyway. Call them." He pressed a little harder against my throat just as I grabbed his wrists and twisted.

I heard the slip of the latch on the door and looked up to see Joelle standing with her arms crossed. "Please check on your brothers. I'm fine." I twisted his arms behind his back and wrapped my own around his. Placing my knee in the bend of his own knee, I forced his legs to bend and then wrapped my legs around his. "I don't want my hands on you, Alex. I want to take my hands off of you, but this is not safe." He swore, and screamed while his body flailed wildly. I knew I wouldn't be able to restrain him much longer.

There was a time when I would have been overcome with anger, hurt, and sadness at this behavior, but it had become commonplace and I couldn't even find a tear to shed. Joelle refused to move, and I looked up at her again, begging her to look away.

"I'm not doing that anymore, Mom. He's going to hurt you, and I can't let anyone else get hurt." It wasn't her responsibility to keep me safe. I knew the harm this was causing her. I knew the hurt she was feeling right at that moment. I didn't want her to watch anymore.

"Please, Joelle, I'm fine." Just then Alexander wiggled free and scrambled to his feet just as my head hit the floor. I shook my head and jumped to my feet only to see him holding a steak knife with his arms wide spread blocking the kitchen. "Joelle." I called.

"I already called, Mom." I heard her say in a voice that was eerily calm. "Yes, this is Joelle. He's my brother. Yes, that's correct. I need a crisis intervention trained officer. He has a knife. He was trying to strangle my mom again."

I kept my eyes on Alexander while I listened to her make the call. "Please put the knife down. I know you don't really want to hurt anyone. I just need you to put it down." I could see the front window just past Alexander's head. One police car pulled directly from the road into my front lawn. Another stopped just behind my van in the driveway.

Just then my phone started beeping with the sound of text message notifications. I knew it would be my neighbors checking in. That was always the worst part, trying to pretend like everything was normal after one of these episodes.

I can't remember what the officer said as he burst through the front door. Alexander dropped the knife onto the counter and stood with his hands up. The anger was gone from his face replaced only with fear. "Why did you do this to me? Mom! Why did you do this to me? Tell them I'm good now. Tell them I'm done." The officer was past me before I could blink and Alexander's arms were swiftly placed into the handcuffs.

The officer moved my son to the front porch. For a moment I felt worried about the neighbors, and then I realized that they were all still talking about the time before, and the time before that. I saw the way they looked at me. I decided I didn't care.

The officer looked at me, and I could see that he felt a measure of my own weariness. "Did he leave a mark?" he asked. He bypassed the typical questions. He already knew my name, the names of all the children present in the home, and my son's name too. It occurred to me that the dogs were sleeping on the floor next to my feet, completely unfazed by the commotion from just moments earlier. That struck me more than the situation itself. The dogs weren't barking and they weren't even standing. They just slept. One officer stepped over our border collie and the awkwardness of his movement moved me to action. I took the dogs by their collars and shut them in the bathroom.

The officer was standing in the dining room with his arms folded. He reminded me that it was the third time they had been there this year.

"I know." I tried to look him in the eye but I felt so ashamed. I choked back tears as I finally found the words that had escaped me for years. "I can't do this anymore. Look at my children." I motioned to my other five children sitting on the stairs just past him. He looked at them. I observed each face and chills went down my spine. They were not crying; they were not afraid; they were fed up. They looked tired and unamused. "My kids think this is normal. They live in this trauma every day. They can't do this anymore. We are all so tired of being afraid. He didn't hurt anyone this time, but what about next time? Will he have to kill someone before we decide we've had enough?"

The officer nodded his head, "I'm going to go talk to probation. I will make sure there is room for him at the detention center. You will need to come straight there to sign release papers."

I agreed and began gathering my things. Mike walked in the door just then. Camille filled him in on what was going on. The officer got approval to take him, and within moments they were driving away. The tears fell then, so many tears. I let the dogs out of the bathroom, and then shut myself inside. I pressed my back to the wall and slid down to sit on the cool tile. When I had no more tears, I rose again and slipped my shoes on. I kissed the kids goodbye, and Mike and I left for the jail.

That night as we arrived home, I did not feel despair, I felt peace. I knew we would be able to sleep through the night without worry. I knew he would be safely locked in a cell. I hated that for him, but I felt relieved all the same. I slept soundly that night and woke the next morning to absolute peace in our home. We had lived in uncertainty for so long that it seemed that no one knew what to do or how to behave in the stillness.

## Behind Bars

I felt the swish of the door behind me and looked up briefly at the four other people in the tiny room. A rather large woman checked her watch and pushed her glasses up her nose. I noticed that she didn't make eye contact either, and I was grateful. An average-size man wearing a flannel shirt, jeans, and work boots stood right behind her with his hands jammed into his pockets and stared at a spot on the wall just behind me. The security guard kept her lips pressed into a thin line, and the observation made me wonder if she had perfected her no-nonsense posture out of necessity or if it came naturally to her.

My husband swiftly signed his name to the sheet before us and placed his keys in the box marked personal belongings. I couldn't look at his face. He spread his arms before the security guard and waited as the metal detector ran over him. I was next, and my watch made the detector buzz, but I was allowed to keep it. I forced a smile and thanked the guard, who told me to turn around as she waved the wand across my back, arms, and legs. Gruffly she told me to wait with my back against the wall and I did. While I waited for the other parents to complete the security check, I tried not to think too much about my surroundings. I felt the sting of tears just at the corners of my eyes and I willed them not to spill over.

The guard closed and locked the second door behind us and led us down the cinder block hallway toward a row of visitation rooms. I could see each of the boys through the small windowed doors. Not my son, not my son, not my son, and then there he was. I walked toward the door and the guard unlocked it for us. My husband and I slipped inside and looked directly into the eyes of our oldest son. His orange-striped jumpsuit only accentuated his shaggy unkempt hair. He smiled at us and sat back easily in his chair. I pulled my own chair close to the table between us. I put my elbows on the table wishing to be closer to him, but he did not move. Mike started the conversation, "How are you doing? Has today been okay for you?" Alexander replied, and from that point on our conversation was easy. We talked about the weather and the recent chill in the air. He told us that he had a long-sleeved shirt that he might put on later and that the blanket on his bed was warm enough. We talked about his brothers and sisters, the dogs, the cat, and the chickens too. It felt natural and unnatural all at the same time.

I checked my watch constantly, willing it to move a little slower. I wanted to talk to him more, but the time flew past, and after what felt like only a moment, the guard was back to unlock the door. I reached over to touch Alexander's hand, and he looked me in the eyes. "Don't cry this time, Mom, okay? You don't have to cry. I'm safe." I squeezed his arm just as he reached over and pulled us both into a hug. I pressed my hands to his back in an effort to remember the feel of my son. I kissed his cheek, knowing that I wouldn't be able to again for a long time.

Mike said, "I love you, son."

"I do too, Dad. I love you too," he replied.

I couldn't say anything at all. I turned to the door and walked away. I watched the other parents enter the common hallway, one common thread between us — sadness. I looked up one last time to see my son in handcuffs returning to his cell. I turned away quickly and stared hard at the guard's back as she led us into the tiny room to gather our belongings and return to the world without our sons.

The sun was high in the sky and surprisingly warm in contrast to the cool wind that had picked up intensity over the course of the morning. Mike spoke first. "I don't actually think he cares. I think he's happier locked up than when he's at home."

I didn't want to admit it, but it was true and always had been. He thrives in structure with very little to no choices. He likes being with people who aren't in his family and does better when the consequences aren't abstract. In detention, the consequence for physical fighting is to be on lockdown for 72 hours inside the cell. He could stop himself from fighting because that was a consequence he was not ready to take. At home we had tried so many ways to create an environment where Alexander could thrive, but instead we just found ourselves frustrated and unsuccessful. We could not ground him to his room because he would leave. We could not lock his door because he would break it down. We could not keep him from jumping out of the window or just plain pushing us out of his way. Our desire was to live at peace with our son and to live in a relationship with him, but the truth had become evident. He did not have the same goals.

I watched the detention center fall behind us in the rearview mirror. My heart felt sadness but not despair. I hated every minute of what was happening with Alexander, but for the first time in a long time I drove toward home with the knowledge that I had five other children there who were ready to live at peace, and they were safe. The knowledge that Alexander could not hurt himself or others for one day was a deep relief.

# CHAPTER 22

# Broken Pieces

Sometimes broken things create more broken things. Have you ever slid your hand across a freshly sanded piece of wood only to find that your finger detected the one sharp piece? Once that piece is lodged firmly in your finger, it is quite difficult to remove. Have you ever broken a glass? It happens in our house quiet often. I would like to say it's the amount of children we have, but the truth is that I'm usually the one who breaks things. I don't' know what it is — carelessness or hurriedness or both. I unload the dishwasher a lot. You would think I would find a more efficient way to return utensils to their proper place. You might even think practice makes perfect. You would be wrong. I unload the dishwasher at least twice a day every day. And at least one of those times, I drop something. I intend to put the plates safely onto their shelf, but with a slip of my fingers I let go and the plate crashes toward the counter, teetering for a split second on the edge. I lunge toward it but my reflexes leave something to be desired, and it completes the descent toward my kitchen floor, shattering into a million pieces. I yell immediately, "Watch your feet!" Why do I do this? Because the once-harmless plate has been broken and now it can break something else.

When Sage was 18 months old, he found this out the hard way. He was playing on our back patio. The night before, Mike and I treated the kids to root beer floats. I was so excited to buy the root beer that comes in the bottles. It just felt more official that way. The summer days had been hot and long, and root beer floats seemed to be just the ticket to refreshment. They were everything I expected. We cleaned up most of our mess before herding the kids to bed. We didn't realize we had missed one of the bottles. Sage was really into kicking things. He just loved to see a ball roll across the floor or a tower of bricks come crashing down.

I was in the kitchen fixing lunch and the girls were watching the boys play in the back yard. All of a sudden I heard the calm, matter-of-fact voice of my nine-year-old daughter. "Mom, Sage kicked one of those bottles and it cut his foot. There is a lot of blood." I turned to look at her face and there were tears welling in her eyes.

"Okay, don't panic," I said to myself or my daughter, I wasn't sure who needed the pep talk more. I ran to the patio and scooped him up. The blood was pouring out of his foot from a cut that ran from his toes all the way to his heal. "Joelle, please get me a towel. Camille, I need you to get the neighbor right now."

I turned Sage upside-down and began wrapping the towel and putting pressure on. Blood soaked through the first towel and Joelle handed me another one. She kept her composure, but I did not. "I'm going to throw up," I admitted with shame. Joelle calmly brought me a bucket. I did throw up, and she dumped it and brought it back for me just in time. The neighbor showed up just then and asked her mom to watch my kids so she could drive us to the hospital. I was grateful and still quite embarrassed. I hugged Joelle and Camille with my free arm, refusing to let go of Sage's foot.

Sage whimpered in my arms and the neighbor used my cell phone to make a call to Mike. He agreed to meet us at the hospital. I held Sage tighter in my arms. My neighbor made conversation, trying to keep my mind off the guilt I was feeling. I appreciated her for it. She kept her eyes on the road, but checked in on me every few minutes. I tried to keep my own eyes off the blood-soaked towel beneath my palm. I pressed with all my might but the stain grew till it reached the span of my fingers. We pulled into the ER drop-off, and she agreed to meet me inside. She started to pull away as I exited the car but then thought better of it and followed me up the walkway and through the sliding doors. I turned and laughed but my voice still felt shaky. "You don't need to follow me."

She shook her head. "Oh, I know I don't." But still she followed until I was safely settled into a chair in the waiting room. I was embarrassed but grateful. The truth was that even I was a little concerned that I might pass out before the day was over. She returned to her car to move it to the parking lot and then met me back inside just as Mike entered the waiting area.

We both thanked her and she left just in time for me to start bawling again. Sage had settled into my arms at that point. We were called back to the room shortly. Mike and I both winced as the nurse cleaned the cut and gave Sage the shots to numb him for the stitches. In the end, he had a tidy row of 15 stitches and a bandage from his toes to his kneecap to protect them. I was astounded that something so small could have done so much damage.

Raising our Alexander was much the same as finding a piece of broken glass with a bare foot. Alexander was sharp and jagged from the time we brought him home. We desired to glue him back together but his sharp edges always ended up injuring us in the process.

When Alexander was 5, he left finger marks on my neck. When he was 6, he bit his therapist. When he was 7, he pushed me down the stairs in the midst of a rage. When he was 8, he threw a broom at me in anger but instead hit his 3-year-old brother in the head, causing a split that took five stitches to mend. When he was 9, he tore a bulletin board off the wall of his classroom and knocked the teacher over when she asked for him to return an iPad. When he was 10, he tore his entire door off the hinges, climbed out of a second-story window, and tried to escape down the trunk of a tiny tree. At 11 years old, he ran at me with a pitchfork. By the time he was 12, his rages were beyond the scope of a therapeutic hold.

When we looked closely at our son, we saw the beauty that was just past the jagged edges. We saw the potential in the brokenness.

When we tore our eyes away from him for a moment, we allowed our other children to come into focus, and they were becoming rougher each day. The sharpness of his words and actions cut each one of us until we were almost too numb to feel the pain.

We became aware of the secondary trauma that had entered into our home. In our effort to heal one child, we had allowed him to terrorize our other children. We were drowning in the pain. Joelle began to become more withdrawn the year she turned 11. We noticed that she was struggling but we couldn't find the words to connect with her. She spent more time in her room and sunk deeper into the books she loved to read. We didn't try to stop it at first. We thought that reading was an appropriate coping skill, but we soon discovered that she was not completing school work and was losing weight as well. We became highly concerned that she didn't have any friends or talking points that involved real people. She became withdrawn and even refused to bathe properly or brush her teeth. Her teachers were beginning to label her as a bad kid for never turning in her homework. We were at a loss.

Late one night, just before Christmas, she admitted that she thought about suicide all the time. She confessed that she lay awake at night trying to convince herself not to take all the pills in the medicine cabinet. We were shocked. Have you ever heard the frog in the pot theory? It goes like this: if you drop a frog into a pot of boiling hot water, it will jump to safety immediately. But if you put a frog into a pot of room temperature water he will sit there happily. If you turn the water up by small degrees, the frog will adjust to the slowly increasing temperature and will not be aware of the danger that lies ahead. The frog will eventually boil to death, never having been aware of the imminent danger all around him. Our family was like that frog, and our home had become the pot. Alexander's behaviors had increased slowly over time. When he was very little, he was disagreeable but manageable. As he became older, he defied safe living and escalated into verbal, emotional, and physical abuse of those closest to him. We were aware that the home was getting a little hotter, but it wasn't until Joelle threw us into the boiling pot that we realized how out of control things actually were.

We spent years trying to find counseling for Joelle as well as continue to manage Alexander's never-ceasing behaviors of aggression. Alexander was frequently in trouble with the police or administration at his school, but I felt the deep desire to advocate for him in a way that would help others understand how his brain had been damaged by drugs, alcohol, and trauma. Mike and I continued to work around the clock to try to create a peaceful haven for our other children in the midst of the chaos that Alexander inevitably created everywhere he went. His sharp edges cut us at every turn.

# CHAPTER 23

# Born Broken

In the years that followed, we began to embrace our new reality. We learned that children who have FASD will never recover, but they are also not a lost cause. We learned that our children who had suffered great trauma in their first families and more trauma in our own, could heal. It was difficult to wake up to the reality of how out of control our life had become, but it was good to finally be awake. Once we realized the reality of our situation, we could all finally begin to heal and embrace the truth of our family and our life. The hard parts of our story will always be here, but there are happy parts too.

Camille not only found her voice, she found a voice for others. Her heart of compassion shines toward those around her. She is doing well in high school and is a good friend to others. She is a problem solver. Even when a task is difficult she is determined to get it right.

Kate and her daughter live right down the street, and we see them often. Kate is hard-working and takes wonderful care of her own child. We love being grandparents. Our two-year-old grand-daughter is a true joy. She loves to stomp in the mud, chase our chickens around the back yard, read stories, and help cook. Her aunts and uncles love to spoil her. Kate is finding her way in this world. Her strength is astounding.

Rachel is married now. She and her husband live close by. They are a support to their brothers and sisters in many ways. Camille and

Joelle love to spend the night at their house watching girly movies and talking. Rachel is thoughtful and trustworthy. She is wise and kind; she is always looking out for others and forgives without a second thought.

Joelle is creative and kind. She is a beautiful singer and writer. She has always struggled to talk about her feelings, but her writing is filled with depth and honesty. She made the honor roll for the first time recently. Her face beamed as she read the award invitation to us over dinner. Every day she grows stronger in her own identity. She feels the emotions of others deeply and I am sure that one day she will be a voice for those who have experienced hardships.

Ezra is about to leave elementary school and enter the world of pre-teens. He is smart and sweet. He is handsome and funny. He is kind to others and always looks out for his younger brothers. He loves to create imaginary games and projects and is a great leader for those younger than he.

Jude is one of the happiest, most content children we know. He loves school and church and anything that involves people. He is particular about how his pants, shoestrings, and bedroom should be, but he never relies on others to make things right for him. He is independent and resourceful. He empathizes with others and is quick to give a hug to anyone who is hurting.

Sage can create something out of nothing. His creativity is boundless. He once spent an entire day pretending to be a dog. He refused to eat with his hands and lapped his cereal out of a bowl using only his tongue. He is filled with wonder and curiosity. He has a sweetness to his exuberance. He will spin like a top all day and then crash into my lap, ready to relax and snuggle.

Alexander sits in a jail cell as I write this. He has had a lot of time to think recently. Every night as we talk on the phone, he reveals more about his own vulnerability. On the weekends we get to see each other under the watchful eye of a guard. Our words are recorded and our contact is limited to one hug just before we exit. My son longs to change. He desires to heal. He is tethered to his past. He is chained to his hurt. He was born into a brokenness that he did not design or deserve. I see something in him though, just beneath the rough surface. I see the light of something that has always been there, hope. The hope that one day my son will embrace the Father who created him. The hope that my son's story will not end here.

It is through my son's brokenness that I have seen my own fractured spirit magnified. For many years I have grieved the loss of what I expected my son to be. I live in a culture that teaches us that if we believe in ourselves, anything is possible. When I was growing up, I was told that I could be anything I put my mind to. I have believed wholeheartedly that with hard-work, perseverance, and a positive attitude, anything can be accomplished. I now believe something else as well. My son has taught me that we all fall short. He has taught me that despite my best intentions, I will never love deeply enough. I will never muster enough joy. My restless spirit will never allow complete peace. I can't always be patient. I am not always kind. I'm not quite as good as I wish. Even my faith is fickle. I desire to be gentle, but my edges are rough. My self-control only lasts for so long. Yes, we are strong and mighty, but in our humanity we also have a frailty. It is in our limitations that we recognize our need for a God who is our strength. It is in our faults that we acknowledge our need for a Savior who redeems us. My own need to heal is amplified when I look into the eyes of my son.

I have hesitated to finish this book. How can a book be complete when there is still so much of the story to tell? Today was my day off but I couldn't relax. I was restless at home and antsy to get moving. I dropped Joelle off at school along with all the other girls in carpool. They weren't very chatty this morning. and that suited me fine. I've had a lot on my mind these past few weeks. I drove without thinking toward my office. I was just about to take the familiar left turn when instead I took a right. I wasn't sure what I was doing at first. I meandered up and down the city streets for a while. It's autumn again and there is nothing I love more than the colorful changing of this season.

I began talking to the Lord about all that was around me. When I pray, I love to talk out loud. I thanked God for the city streets and for the warmth of my car heater. I thanked God for the sun and for my family. Then I thanked God for something that surprised me even as it came out of my mouth. I thanked God for the deep sadness I feel for Alexander. In this sorrow, I feel even more deeply my love for him. It struck me then as I marveled at the tree-lined streets. Autumn is a season of loss, but it is filled with the beauty of renewal that is to come. The leaves are changing; they are dying to what they once were. Green turns to gold as the former fades away. Brilliant reds and oranges replace the hues of the summer. The wind kicked up as I turned down a timeworn brick road. The stems released their grip from the branches above me, and a shower of color filled the sky. I pull the car to the curb and watched, mesmerized by the beauty. The leaves swirled around me. Free. No longer anchored to their old self but transformed into something new. No longer hindered by what they are leaving behind. I looked up and down the street. Empty. I was the solitary spectator to this spectacular display. The artistry was for my eyes only. I serve a God who pours out His goodness even when I am the only one watching. He does not count the cost, even when the expense is everything.

For now, I too am letting go. I will not hold on to the past. I will not hold on to what I hoped would be. I will allow myself to let go so that I may also become a part of my Father's brilliant artistry. I will let go so that the rest of my son's story may be written by the God who created him.

FASD — Fetal Alcohol Spectrum Disorder is the umbrella term for any of the effects that can occur when a person is exposed to alcohol before birth.

FAS — Fetal Alcohol Syndrome

ARND — Alcohol Related Neurodevelopmental Disorder

PFAS — Partial Fetal Alcohol Syndrome

ND-PAE — Neurobehavioral Disorder Associated with Prenatal Alcohol Exposure

Behavioral Symptoms of FASD
  Difficulty understanding abstract concepts like time and money
  Difficulty planning for and following directions involving two or more steps
  Lack of ability to apply consequences to actions
  Difficulty with working memory, storing and retrieving information
  Difficulty regulating emotions. Emotions may swing to extremes and may have difficulty regaining composure.
  May show lack of remorse
  May need outside influence to motivate

# Resources

If you are looking for support, here are some resources I suggest.

nofas.org

*The Connected Child* by Karen Purvis

ntiupstream.com

therefreshconference.org

onethankfulmom.com

ellenstumbo.com

Author connections:

confessionsofanadoptiveparent.com

facebook.com/confessionsofanadoptiveparent